Transforming Truths

Modern daily Christian inspirations for growth & positive transformation

Transforming Truths
Modern daily Christian inspirations
for growth & positive transformation

By

Melanie Schurr

Inspirations within have appeared at DailyWisdom.com
Scripture quotations from RSV and NIV
Visit the author at www.MelanieSchurr.com
ISBN: 978-0-6151-4938-7

Dedications

As always, all the glory and honor goes to God, for without Him, I would be nothing. I thank Him for the knowledge and understanding He has nurtured over time within me, and for allowing me to be a tiny instrument within His hand.

To Edward, my loving husband and best-friend of over twenty-three years who has been an unwavering source of support and encouragement. Your love fills me!

To my daughter, Lindsey, whose thoughtfulness, love and appreciation of me means more than you could ever know!

To my son, Aaron, who recently returned from being stationed in Iraq within the United States Army. Your bravery, strength and courage astounds me! Thanks to you, I have learned to better understand complete unconditional love.

To my (deceased) brother, Nicky. Thank you (and God) for those last few precious years. I know you felt my love and respect, and I felt yours. I still do, and this comforts & sustains me while I await our heavenly reunion.
(continued)

To my mother, Joan, for being the only family member outside of my own immediate family, to not only read all of my books, but show genuine interest in something that is very important to me. Your support means much!

To my father, Tony, who provided me with a living example of what it means to be a man of good character. Thank you for that example!

To the folks at *The Gospel Communications Network* and *Daily Wisdom* who have allowed me to share God's good news for over twelve yrs. Thank you for giving me a regular outlet so I can do what I love, and to which gives my life more meaning & purpose.

And, to the wonderful readers: I am continually humbled and grateful, because, without your questions and positive comments, I would not have had the idea in the first place to publish that first book. Your interest in and support of *Daily Wisdom*, & my own ministry, is wholeheartedly appreciated.

Forward

Transform:

1 a : *to change in composition or structure* **b :** *to change the outward form or appearance of* **c :** *to change in character or condition*

I have always had a significantly stronger interest in non-fiction books as opposed to fiction. I suppose this is because, while it is nice to be entertained by fantasy, the larger part of me seeks to learn, grow and hopefully, steadily improve so that my life can be the best possible. For me, transformation is absolutely necessary, for how sad it would be if I remained at the same maturity and general operating level that I was at age eighteen. If such was the case, I'd still be repeating the same mistakes, stuck in dead-end relationships and wasting my time with what I now know to be meaningless frivolities.

"And Jesus increased in wisdom and stature, and in favour with God and man." -Luke 2:52

Unfortunately, there are some people in the world who do not yet appreciate the beauty and necessity of positive change; and to admit the need for transformation is likened to admitting failure.

I know a woman who lost her relationship with her only (adult) child simply because she could not bring herself to admit the wrongs she had clearly committed against her son and his own family. How simple the words, "I'm sorry. I really screwed up," are, yet, for many individuals, the mere idea they could, heaven forbid, be less than perfect, is such an excruciating thought that it is seemingly easier and less painful to just give up, ignore the problem, and live in denial.

Man can be a terribly self-centered and proud creature, and while a certain amount of confidence and self-esteem is healthy and required, an excess of pride can be a real destroyer. What this mother's action (or lack thereof), revealed, is that retaining her pride and saving face was more important than preserving her relationship with her only child.

A precious gift a friend gave me in my late teens was the ability to say "I'm sorry." Before that time, I would make excuses, beat around the bush and drag my feet in the dirt; anything to avoid admitting I had done wrong. I'm still not fully sure why it was such an objectionable thing but I suspect it was because if I admitted to others that I had made a bad decision, used poor judgment, or engaged in improper activity, they might see me as stupid, incapable or low.

The fact is, we *all* want to be loved, but, unless we learn to first love ourselves, how can we be expected to well-love others? As such, we need to be kind to ourselves; giving ourselves permission to be merciful and forgiving toward our *own* flaws, weaknesses and transgressions.

Why?

Because we <u>all</u> have them, and <u>no one</u> but God is completely perfect and without sin. Thus so, to try and cleave to this imaginary status of perfection merely lowers one to the position of fool. We kid no one, for even behind the fixed smiles, impressive degrees, and picture-perfect homes, our negative aspects and sins always have a way of creeping out and revealing themselves, especially when we think no one is listening or watching.

I used to know a middle-aged woman who, from outer appearance, seemed like a very nice lady. She dressed conservatively, spoke softly in public, had excellent manners, and was obviously, well-educated. Yet, as we became more friendly, and she grew more comfortable with me, thus letting her guard down, I began to see a very ugly side to her. Others noticed too, and tried to bring it to her attention, but change was impossible because she refused to take a good, hard look in the mirror. Eventually, she lost most of her old friends, the respect of some family members, and even her marriage.

Assuming there is no such thing as reincarnation, life is a one-shot deal. Once we die we cannot turn back the hands of time to correct our mistakes. This is it: now or never. Either we can go about life like an ostrich with its head in the sand; oblivious and in-denial of what is real about our character and life, or we can bravely march before that mirror and see ourselves for who we really are, warts and all.

No, it's not always easy to admit we have a shortcoming, or some facet to our character could use some tweaking, but, as with jumping into a pool, once you take that first plunge, you will see that most of the hesitation we hold is much ado about nothing. And, as with all things in life, the more we do it, the easier it becomes. Using the pool analogy again, as difficult as it may be to imagine, a time will come when you too are able to shout to the next person, "Come on in! The water's fine!"

The water is fine, but it is not the chlorine-enhanced pool water I speak of, but the purifying and cleansing waters of God's merciful forgiveness to those who call out to Him in repentance. If we were perfect, God would not have sent His Son, Jesus Christ, to die on the cross for our sins.

Many years ago, when I first began to share my personal testimony of how my faith in God helped deliver me from a period of dabbling in drugs, alcohol and general ungodly living, which included the pain of a past abortion, I immediately noticed that being honest and talking about these bad decisions was not only a freeing cathartic, but also provided great fulfillment in knowing that my story can help teach and reach others.

Let's face it, people tend to not like to talk too much about their flaws, weaknesses and mistakes. We'd much rather toot our own horn about our achievements and strengths. However, I found that when I used the example of my own past flubs, people felt much more comfortable in sharing their own because they knew I could relate.

Now and then a reader will write seeking advice. As I often tell them, I am not a therapist, but what I can do is listen, join them in prayer, and share what works for me.

What works?

The sheer desire to change: to be a better person, and more pleasing in God's eyes.

Certainly, we may also wish to better ourselves

for other reasons, such as health, family, job, and finances, but when our primary motivating factor is God and the desire for godliness, that is when the really exciting stuff begins to happen!

What stuff?

Spiritual growth! Spiritual blessings!

"What's so important about that?" you ask.

Very important! That is, if you want a life which consists of love, joy, peace, patience, kindness, goodness, faithfulness, gentleness and self-control!

"But the fruit of the Spirit is love, joy, peace, patience, kindness, goodness, faithfulness, gentleness and self-control." -Galations 5:22

If you are becoming more loving, joyful, kind, more self-controlled, etc., then these are signs that spiritual growth is genuinely occurring in your life.

For a moment, let's just focus on the above two *'fruits of the spirit'*, peace and joy. Can you imagine a life void of genuine peace and joy?

I can't, yet how saddening it is to know that many people live their entire life not knowing the calm of peace that passes all understanding, and the depth of joy so rich one does not need external stimuli or special circumstance to bring this forth.

Within the Bible, God calls us to positive change and transformation:

*"And be not conformed to this world: but be ye **transformed** by the renewing of your mind, that ye may prove what is that good, and acceptable, and perfect, will of God." -Romans 12:2*

*"Therefore, if anyone is in Christ, he is a **new creation**; the old has gone, the new has come!"*
                              -2 Corinthians 5:17

Metamorphosis:

1 a : change of physical form, structure, or substance especially by supernatural means b : a striking alteration in appearance, character, or circumstances
2 : a typically marked and more or less abrupt developmental change in the form or structure of an

*animal (as a butterfly or a frog) occurring
subsequent to birth or hatching*

When I think of transformation, I am reminded
of the butterfly who goes through four stages
in its life. Each stage is very different from the
others. The entire cycle of stages is called
metamorphosis.

The butterfly begins its life as a small egg.
The larva hatches from the egg. Butterfly (and
moth) larvae are typically called caterpillars.
When a caterpillar has finished growing, it
forms a pupa. From the outside, the pupa looks
as if it's resting. But inside, every part of the
caterpillar is changing. Most of its organs and
other body parts dissolve and re-form into the
organs, tissues, limbs and wings of the adult
butterfly. Butterfly pupae are called
chrysalises, or what some people refer to as
cocoons.

When the pupa has finished changing, it molts
one last time and emerges as a beautiful adult
butterfly.

Humans go through stages of life as well, and
it is a normal and good thing that we change in
mind and body during our journey as infant,
adolescent, and adult. However, we are more
than just physical beings. We are, or have been
created to be complete in mind, body and
spirit. As someone once said, *"We are not flesh*

and blood beings here on a spiritual journey, but spiritual beings on a flesh and blood journey." In short, we came from God, and it is His desire for all men to come back to Him. Sadly, not all men desire this for themselves.

The butterfly analogy may also be used when contemplating what occurs within the death of the Christian. The flesh and blood body is cast away, and the spirit is free to emerge as a sole entity; back to whence it came, God. Just as the caterpillar's goal and final destination is to be transformed into a butterfly, the Christian's goal, destination and true glory is spiritual.

How do we know this?

Because, as the Bible states, flesh is corruptible. As we grow old, it ages, and eventually begins to fail. Flesh was not made to last indefinitely. Spirit, on the other hand, is not corruptible, and is everlasting.

"So also is the resurrection of the dead. It is sown in corruption; it is raised in incorruption:
It is sown in dishonour; it is raised in glory: it is sown in weakness; it is raised in power:
It is sown a natural body; it is raised a spiritual body. There is a natural body, and there is a spiritual body." -I Corinthians 15:42-44

*"And as we have borne the image of the earthy, we
shall also bear the image of the heavenly.
Now this I say, brethren, that flesh and blood
cannot inherit the kingdom of God; neither doth
corruption inherit incorruption.
Behold, I shew you a mystery; We shall not all
sleep, [die] but we shall all be changed,
In a moment, in the twinkling of an eye, at the last
trump: for the trumpet shall sound, and the dead
shall be raised incorruptible, and we shall be
changed.
For this corruptible must put on incorruption, and
this mortal must put on immortality."*
-I Corinthians 15:49-53

When my brother, Nicky, unexpectedly passed
away at age 48, while I was utterly saddened
and broken-hearted, my grief was lessened by
the knowledge that Nick was only gone in
body, but not in spirit. My pain and tears was
for the earthly loss, but of the spiritual, I knew
he was now at peace and with God, and that
one day we would see each other again. As a
little reminder of his transformation, and
perhaps a comforting memorial that would
stay with me always, I had a tattoo of a
butterfly with beautiful and colorful
outstretched wings placed upon each of my
ankles. I will not get into the whole right or
wrong tattoo debate at this time, but I will say
that if a memorial-type tattoo can help
someone lessen their grief, that is between

them and God, and it is up to no one else to judge.

The Bible also speaks of another type of transformation which must take place before we can enter into the kingdom of God. It is an often misunderstood term that relates to all Believers, yet somewhere along the line society, in its often Scriptural ignorance, tends to only relate it to a certain sect of Christianity. The term which describes this mandated change is *"born again."*

Let us see what God's word has to say on this topic:

"In reply Jesus declared, "I tell you the truth, no one can see the kingdom of God unless he is born again. ""-John 3:3

"You should not be surprised at my saying, 'You must be born again.'"-John 3:7

"...see that ye love one another with a pure heart fervently:
Being born again, not of corruptible seed, but of incorruptible, by the word of God, which liveth and abideth for ever.
For all flesh is as grass, and all the glory of man as the flower of grass. The grass withereth, and the flower thereof falleth away:
But the word of the Lord endureth for ever."
-I Peter 1:22-25

*"For you have been **born again**, not of perishable seed, but of imperishable, through the living and enduring word of God."-I Peter 1:23*

A year or so ago, a feisty elderly woman quipped, "Weren't they born once that they have to be born again?! I don't need to be born *again!*"

Similar question was posed to Jesus during his time on earth, and here is how he responded:

"How can a man be born when he is old?" Nicodemus asked. "Surely he cannot enter a second time into his mother's womb to be born!"
*Jesus answered, "I tell you the truth, no one can enter the kingdom of God unless he is born of water and the Spirit. Flesh gives birth to flesh, but the Spirit gives birth to spirit. You should not be surprised at my saying, 'You must be **born again.'** The wind blows wherever it pleases. You hear its sound, but you cannot tell where it comes from or where it is going. So it is with everyone born of the Spirit."*
"How can this be?" Nicodemus asked.
"You are Israel's teacher," said Jesus, "and do you not understand these things? I tell you the truth, we speak of what we know, and we testify to what we have seen, but still you people do not accept our testimony. I have spoken to you of earthly things

*and you do not believe; how then will you believe if
I speak of heavenly things? No one has ever gone
into heaven except the one who came from heaven —
the Son of Man. Just as Moses lifted up the snake in
the desert, so the Son of Man must be lifted up, that
everyone who believes in him may have eternal life.
"For God so loved the world that he gave his one
and only Son, that whoever believes in him shall not
perish but have eternal life. For God did not send
his Son into the world to condemn the world, but to
save the world through him. Whoever believes in
him is not condemned, but whoever does not believe
stands condemned already because he has not
believed in the name of God's one and only Son.
This is the verdict: Light has come into the world,
but men loved darkness instead of light because
their deeds were evil. Everyone who does evil hates
the light, and will not come into the light for fear
that his deeds will be exposed. But whoever lives by
the truth comes into the light, so that it may be seen
plainly that what he has done has been done
through God." -John 3:9-20*

In more simple terms, Christ clearly tells us
that baptism by water is not enough, for water
is still only water. We must be baptized by the
Holy Spirit, and as the above Scripture states,
this is done by our sincere faith and belief in
God and His Son, Jesus Christ.

That's it?

Well, yes and no.

Simply saying "I believe," doesn't make it so, for belief is <u>action</u>.

Here's an example:

A man says he believes stealing is wrong, yet, a week later he is arrested for robbing a bank. Obviously, this mans words were hollow and insincere, and his actions proved this.

The same is true with our acclaimed belief in God and His Son, Jesus Christ. You've got to walk the walk, not just talk the talk. Meaning, our faith becomes more than mere lip service or something we only pull out on Sundays, or when we know someone is watching or listening. This is why many Christians refer to "inviting Jesus into their hearts" because where the heart truly is, the actions follow.

Inviting Christ into a heart full of sin and ungodliness is like asking a house-guest to stay in a filthy and smelly cockroach-ridden room that is uninhabitable. As such, along with our admission of belief is typically a renunciation of sin so that we can not only give to God a temple that is more suitable for His Divine presence, but prove to God that our faith is important and real. Now, if that isn't a transformation, I don't know what is!

The following is an example of a prayer someone desiring to be born-again might say:

God, I want to know You better, and thus, I invite You into my heart and life. Show me, God, what it is You require from me so that my life may be more pleasing to You. I ask You to please forgive me of any sins I have not repented of, and to wash me clean with Your love and mercy. Create in me a new heart, God; one that thirsts for truth and goodness. Make me a new creation and fill me with Your holy spirit.

I believe You sent Your Son, Jesus Christ to die on the cross for my sins, God, and so that I may have eternal life.

I ask You for this in the name of Your Son, Jesus Christ.

Transformations

I recall when I was a teenager, there was this very tough girl in town; a biker-type female who wore leather, swore like a sailor, loved to instigate fights, drink, do drugs, and generally, just scare off people with her hard as nails exterior. Admittedly, I was afraid of her because she had harassed and assaulted a friend of mine, and like everyone else, I had heard the stories of how this tough girl threatened this guy, or hit that gal.

Several years later, this same young woman came in to a restaurant I was working at. She called me over, but as she looked so different, I didn't immediately recognize her because this person now before me looked so sweet and gentle.

The young woman told me who she was; assuring me that I didn't need to be fearful of her anymore because she is no longer the same person. She then apologized for any wrongs she may have committed against me or my friends, and went on to explain she had repented of her former ways, and was now a Christian!

Within my life I have witnessed some amazing transformations, but this one in particular I will never forget because it was miraculously dramatic. The situation also taught me a life-long lesson, which is, to not be so quick to judge.

I wondered to myself, "Why hadn't 'I' shared my faith with this person before?"

The mistake I made was that I wrongly assumed she could never be interested in spiritual matters because her personality, at the time, seemed so contrary to all that Christ stood for.

You can bet I never made that mistake again.

I should have known better; understood that with God, all things are possible!

All people carry within them a story. Sometimes that story reveals a past filled with pain, abuse or neglect. Often times, all it takes to help an individual rise up and overcome, is for someone to take the time to care, or to point them in the right direction.

Yes, I have seen cold and hardened exteriors melt away through the warmth of God's love.

Today, take hold of God's outstretched hand so that you too can be transformed as only He and His merciful grace can do.

Garbage Mouth

"Do not let any unwholesome talk come out of your mouths, but only what is helpful for building others up according to their needs, that it may benefit those who listen."
-Ephesians 4:29

𝓜any people today suffer from a terrible affliction called "garbage mouth." The sad thing about it is that many are oblivious to their own sickness.

"Oh, swearing is just part of the culture now," says Tyrell, "Everybody is doing it!"

"Don't be so uptight!" shouts Tonya, "It's just words!"

Our world has such diverse and beautiful languages. Open a dictionary and millions of words to express how we think, feel and act are depicted within the pages. So too do those who hold diplomas and degrees pride themselves in their higher education.

We claim to be a civilized nation, and yet, to listen to how we often chose to express ourselves; opting cheap, gutter and street language, one would never know we are the intelligent and advanced people we claim.

"Hey! It's not about brains, it's about sounding cool!" says Marvin, "All the hip rappers and gangstas talk like that!"

Wanting to be popular, liked, and be part of the "in-crowd" is understandable. However, is swearing so important that we are willing to place it even before our own character and standards, not to mention the fact those around us may find it very offensive and insulting?

The truth of the matter is that not everyone finds curse words funny, cute, or cool. More importunately, in His word, the Bible, God clearly tells us, *"If anyone considers himself religious and yet does not keep a tight rein on his tongue, he deceives himself and his religion is worthless."* (James 1:26) We are also told, *"With the tongue we praise our Lord and Father, and with it we curse men, who have been made in God's likeness. Out of the same mouth come praise and cursing."* (James 3:9-10)

Dear friend, words DO mean things, even when we may think they don't. Calling a child an idiot can hurt to the core, and when an angry husband shouts to his wife, "You never do anything right! Why don't you just crawl away and die!" you can bet those words also hurt just as much as a physical blow.

Friends, just because curse words don't seem

to hurt 'you, ' doesn't mean there aren't others in ear-shot who are silently affected. More importantly, GOD hears, and it is important enough for Him to have made sure this message was put forth in the Bible many times. *"The good man brings good things out of the good stored up in his heart, and the evil man brings evil things out of the evil stored up in his heart. For out of the overflow of his heart his mouth speaks." - Luke 6:45*

As the above Bible verse reveals, the language we use shows others (and God) the type of person we are.

Let us love one another, as God commands; not just by deed, but even in the sweetness and thoughtfulness of our speech.

Prayer: Heavenly Father, I am tired of feeling like a polluted vessel who is full of corruption. It is my desire to be washed clean so that I may begin anew, and be an honor to You, as well as my self. This I ask in the name of Your Son, Jesus Christ. Amen.

Positive Change

"... let God transform you into a new person by changing the way you think. Then you will know what God wants you to do, and you will know how good and pleasing and perfect his will really is."
- Romans 12:2

*C*hange can be frightening at times because it entails a breaking away of what is familiar in order to step into something new. That new thing may be a relocation to another state, joining a new club, meeting new friends, or trying a new hair style. Changes can also run the gamut, from change to the better, or change for the worse.

Think of how giving in to ungodly acts can change someone. Consider the person who steals from their employer, thus loses their job due to what their boss justly regards as a crime. Or what about the individual who gives in lust by getting unhealthily close to a member of the opposite sex then having an extra-marital affair to which ends up destroying their marriage?

God <u>does</u> call us to change; to open our wings like a butterfly who has transformed from a caterpillar, and broken free of his cocoon. God desires this beautiful transformation so that we can live up to the potential He calls us to: new creations who thirst for God's good and pleasing ways. Our Creator wants our desire to be to please Him, not man, because what society may deem as OK, is not always OK is God's eyes. Man may say it's OK to have a little fling as long as no one finds out, but God defines adultery as sin. So too does man often support a spirit of vengeance by wanting to return jab for jab and blow for blow, but God calls us to love one another and treat each other as you yourself wish to be treated.

While change can be disconcerting at times, there is no need to fear with our Heavenly Father. He is our loving Dad who only wants what is best for us so that we may not only be approved in His sight, but live more joyously and peacefully.

Take His hand and make a positive change today.

Get Motivated!

I must admit a small pet peeve I have; people who whine and complain about how bad this or that is, yet refuse to take positive action to change anything. For example, I'm sure we all can think of at least one or two friends or relations who express displeasure in their weight, yet when you ask them if they are going to exercise and eat healthy so they can change what distresses them they have a whole list of reasons why they can't. "Oh, I hate exercising!" says one lady, "And besides, where would I find the time?" Or, another person may say, "I'd miss my nightly pizza and chocolate donuts! Fruits and vegetables just don't cut it for me."

Then of course, there are the people who say they are willing to do something about it, but its always at a later date. "I'll start my diet tomorrow, but for tonight, its fried chicken, country gravy, potato salad and fudge brownies," claims another. Of course, when tomorrow comes, the deed is put off for the next day and the next, and years later, nothing has changed except the bathroom scale that now reads 300 pounds.

The above is only one example of how we often procrastinate because we are unable to motivate (ourselves). The issue here is not dieting, but can relate to any corner of our life that is robbing us of mind, body and/or spirit good health. The unhealthiness may rest in negative mind-sets, destructive relationships, even our lack of relationship with God.

A better life does not just fall into ones lap. It comes when we have a clear vision in mind, and work toward a specific goal. What is necessary, however, is our own motivation; the ability to inwardly tell ourselves, "This is what I want, and this is what I am going to work for until it finally happens!"

The same thing is true with ones relationship with God. Why put off for tomorrow what you can have today?

Don't wait till you are on your death-bed to call out to God. Let Him bless your life as only He alone can do.

Get motivated and invite God in your heart today!

Good-bye to Otis

A day I hoped would never occur, has. Our beloved canine companion of sixteen years, Otis, will be "put to sleep" tomorrow. It is, of course, something I do not want to do, but believe must be done due to Otis' degrading heath which has rendered it virtually impossible for him to function normally. He cannot walk, eat or drink without assistance. His eye-sight is poor, and his incontinence is becoming more frequent.

Upon discussing our dog's fate within our family circle, it was finally decided that Otis has been too loyal and good a friend to allow him to suffer further, and not have the quality of life he would want. We also determined that if this was going to have to happen, we desire it to be done as gently and peacefully as possible. As such, our veterinarian will make a house call tomorrow, and while surrounded and embraced by the people who love him the most, we will say so-long to our wonderful furry friend for one last time.

Saying good-bye to someone or something that we are attached to, and very familiar with, is not always easy. However, as with our situation with Otis, there are times in life it is simply necessary to let go.

Releasing the grip of sin within our lives can be like this as well, for we often get used to giving in to every ungodly temptation and fleshly desire. We may want to stop, and turn over a new leaf, but we may not know how, or we just aren't sure we are willing to do what it takes to be pleasing in God's sight.

Prayer: "Dear God, I admit that I am weak, and that I have sometimes failed You. I have been living for myself, and making bad choices. I want to know You better, God, and I believe You can give me the strength I need to turn my life around. I know it will not be easy, but it is something I now see I must do if I am to be saved. I ask this of You, in the name of Your Son, Jesus Christ. Amen."

Welcome, Spencer!

*W*hen our beloved dog of sixteen years, Otis, died, our nineteen year old daughter, Lindsey, and I agreed that there would never again be another dog in our home. "I never want to have to deal with the pain on losing another dog again, " I told her. She affirmed, saying, "No dog could take the place of Otis!"

Our position was firm, and even when the veterinarian mentioned to us that the best thing we could do to help with our sense of loss was to get another dog, I felt insulted, and thought her quite emotionally cold to even think we could possibly even wish to replace such a loyal and good friend.

Today, I feel a bit silly writing the above because we have a new addition to our family. An adorable little Cocker Spaniel named "Spencer."

Getting a new canine companion was the last thing on our mind, but the death of Otis revealed how much joy he had brought to our family. Without him, there was no one to get excited when I walked in the door during the afternoon, and the other family members were off to work. Nor was there no one there to issue me a lick or a cuddle, or someone to encourage me to go outside for a walk because they needed some exercise. Likewise, during those occasional late nights when my husband had to work over-time, or go out of town, no one was there to provide me that sense of protection and security.

Our new dog, Spencer, is not meant to replace Otis, for that is impossible because he was one of a kind! Likewise, Spencer is a unique dog all himself, and will be appreciated for his special qualities as well. Once again though, our home has that same sense of life and energy, and Spencer's presence clearly brings a smile to all our faces!

Today's Daily Wisdom is not about dogs, dealing with loss, or even the preciousness of life. The deeper message I hope to convey is one of the impossible being possible. Things we thought never being able to occur, happening.

Just as I never thought I'd ever own another dog, likewise, there are people who think that a difficult life situation they are in can not change. Or, a mother and father may think it impossible for their teen to break the addiction of drugs, or build a new relationship with Christ.

However, just as I proved myself wrong, faith in God and surrendering to His awesome abilities CAN make the impossible possible!

Prayer: "Dear God, please help me to trust You better. Allow me to place my life and all its various facets within Your capable hands because You can see the bigger picture that I cannot. Help me to see that You can make the ugly, beautiful, and the sinful, spotless. All that is needed is our faith, and Your mercy. This I ask in the name of Your Son, Jesus Christ. Amen."

(FYI: Shortly after the writing of this devotional, the author & her family welcomed a second dog, named "Lady-Bug," into their family!)

Who Needs A Gang?

*S*tudies reveal that most gang members come from broken homes.

States Ramone, "My father was gone…doing time in jail, and my mother was a drug addict. Most days I got my self off for school because she was passed out on the couch from the night before."

Dino replies, "My mother had me when she was only sixteen years old. By time I was ten years old, she had been married three times. The last guy she married was abusive, so I took off as soon as I could."

Jane agrees, "I knew who my real father was, but I guess he never wanted to spend any time with me. My mother did the best she could as a single parent, but I spent many nights alone because mom had to work two jobs just to make ends meet."

It is believed that gang members join gangs to feel a sense of unity and belonging, and because they realize there is strength in numbers. Such members have expressed they did not feel this sense of "family" within the home, so they subconsciously sought it out elsewhere.

How good it would be if all children, especially those from broken homes, could know and find comfort in the words of the Bible which reveal the very special position those who believe in God have. A person may not have an earthly father who is present in their life, but as children of God, we have a heavenly Father!

"Behold what manner of love the Father hath bestowed upon us, that we should be called children of God; and such we are. For this cause the world knoweth us not, because it knew him not."
-I John 3:1

How wonderful it would also be if such young people tempted to seek a sense of belonging and identity within gang life, could feel strength from knowing they are "heirs of God" and "fellow heirs with Christ," which basically means, we, as Believers, have the best daddy and family of all!

"The Spirit Himself testifies with our spirit that we are children of God, and if children, heirs also, heirs of God and fellow heirs with Christ, if indeed we suffer with Him so that we may also be glorified with Him." -Romans 8:16-17

My dear friend, why seek goodness amongst evil? God, your loving Father is eager and willing to embrace you in to His arms and feed you with His living word.

Handling Depression

"Hope in God, for I shall yet praise Him For the help of His countenance." -Psalm 42:5

30 to 40 million Americans are reported to suffer from depression.

If you think you may be one of those people who also has it, keep in mind that society tends to use the word "depression" to cover everything from sadness or disappointment over failing a test to the overwhelming sense of hopelessness and despair that some people say have caused them to contemplate suicide.

Oftentimes, one's depression has underlying causes that are not physical, chemical or hormonal, but may be the result of something depressing going on in your life. By working on the cause of the problem, these feelings of sadness and frustration may fade.

No one's life is truly perfect, but by not allowing ourselves to get so dragged down by every negative situation or hurtful word that may come our way, we can have better control over our own peace and happiness.

Why?

Because while we can't control others, we CAN control how we allow others to affect us. As such, if we are living a good and godly life, and have no reason to feel the heavy burden and consequence of sin and the separation it causes between God and ourselves, then let us instead sing praises to Him, and be thankful for all God has blessed us with!

"What about antidepressant pills?" asks Mary.

God has allowed mankind to learn about many medical marvels and tools. If we don't have a problem taking daily vitamins to stay healthy, or getting a yearly flu shot to ward of sickness, or even to have a life-saving operation when needed, then no one should feel shame or embarrassment when medication is prescribed for a true chemical imbalance. Oftentimes, even when the depression may not be hormonal, a doctor may temporarily prescribe anti-depressant medication so that the patient can come to a better emotional place where they are more able to tackle an unresolved issue or root cause of their depressed feelings. Perhaps they may have a history of abuse, or feel worthless because they were given up for adoption as a child.

Prayer: Dear God, you know I've been feeling very depressed lately. Please help me to see truth for what it is; show me the reality of why I feel this heaviness upon my heart so that I can walk upon the road to healing. Today, I place my life in Your hand's, God, and I trust You to be a loving Father. This I ask in the name of Your son, Jesus Christ. Amen"

Removing Eye Specks

"*If* I was a single parent, I'd do much better for my child than that woman has done for hers!" boasted Joyce, a tough as nails woman in her mid-sixties. "But then again, what do you expect from a divorcee? " she continued.

The comments should have shocked Eileen, her neighbor, but after twenty years of living side by side, Eileen was used to Joyce's negative rants and blatant insensitivity.

"I recall the first time I met Joyce," recalls Eileen. "She had just moved into the neighborhood and I went to her home to welcome her. She whined the whole time; telling me what she didn't like about these people, or what irritated her about those people. I have never met someone who had so little empathy."

Real life application: Unfortunately, there a lot of people like Joyce around; some who even claim to be Christians. Perhaps at times, even you or I may sound like Joyce; pointing a finger at those individuals who we believe are not as good as us for one reason or another. Maybe they have a problem with alcohol or drugs. Or maybe they have made some mistakes in their past which they repented of, but they are still facing the consequences of their former poor choices.

In the Bible, Jesus Christ, the son of God, had something to say about such people who would go around finding flaws in others while paying no attention to their own. In essence, He said that before we point a guilty finger at others, we should first look within our own lives because, while we may be worrying about a spec in our neighbors eye, we ourselves may have a beam in our own!

"Why do you look at the speck that is in your brother's eye, but do not notice the log that is in your own eye? "Or how can you say to your brother, 'Let me take the speck out of your eye,' and behold, the log is in your own eye? "You hypocrite, first take the log out of your own eye, and then you will see clearly to take the speck out of your brother's eye."-Matthew 7: 3-5

My dear friend, are we really that much better than the people we go about condemning? The Bible says that we ALL have sinned and fallen short, and that NO man is truly righteous of his own accord, and that it is only by the grace of God that we, His children, are saved.

"…for all have sinned and fall short of the glory of God." Romans 3:23

The next time you want to look down upon a dirty homeless man begging in the street, or pointing an accusatory finger at the divorcee who is struggling to raise her child alone, remember that God is willing to be gracious and compassionate to you, and perhaps, it would suit us better to follow His lead so we can truly be living examples of His word.

"In everything, therefore, treat people the same way you want them to treat you, for this is the Law and the Prophets."-Matthew 7:12

In My Father's Shoes

I was thinking of my dad the other day, most likely because we reside at opposite ends of the country, and I am unable to see him as much as I would like.

What I am trying to say is, I miss him.

Dad is now in his late seventies, and needs some assistance in daily living. However, there was a time when 'he' was the one doing the helping; doing the best he could to support his family while also caring for a very large yard, garden, and all those mysterious projects in his work area that kept him constantly hammering, painting, and piddling around the basement.

When dad was in work mode, he wore the same pair of thick leather boots year after year. The well-broken into boots were spattered with paint, tar and grass stains. When my mother would send me into the basement to fetch a jar of string beans or pickles she had canned and stored there, rather than put on a pair of my own shoes, I would instead slip on dad's old boots despite the fact they were dirty, much too big for my tiny feet, and clearly not a female's shoe.

Off I would clomp and slide with an ear to ear grin on my face.

There was something about those old boots of dad's that seemed special to me at the time. Perhaps Sigmund Freud might say it was a childish attempt at trying to follow in my father's footsteps; a sign of admiration for a man I deeply respected and loved.

When I think of this quaint childhood story, I am also reminded that, in essence, Christ also wants us to put on *His* shoes by following in *His* footsteps.

My dear friend, let us give our children a good role model who they can look up to, respect and love. And, may we always look heaven-ward, keeping our head, heart, and eyes on Him who is deserving to be called King of King, and Lord of Lords.

Don't Decay!

I read something very interesting about our bodies the other day. States Dr. Henry S. Lodge, *"When you don't exercise, your muscles let out a steady trickle of chemicals that tell every cell to decay, day after day after day."*

"Whoa!" I thought to myself. "I better start being more physically active!"

Did you know the same thing can happen to us spiritually?

We may start off as all excited for the Lord, and we're ready to turn over a new leaf, but then something comes up, and your good intentions are eventually forgotten. Or, perhaps you are already a Christian, but your neglect of your faith started with putting off your daily prayers, which then progress into a lie here, and an unkind word there. Before you know it, a subtle snow-ball effect is taking place, and your thoughts are becoming more lustful, your actions less loving, and your heart no longer desiring to put God first.

My friend, just as our bodies can become physically sick, so too can we become spiritually ill. And just as laziness can lead to soft muscles which have atrophied, likewise do our spirits suffer when we do not properly nurture it.

Prayer: "Dear God, create in me a new heart; one that hungers for Your word, and thirsts for Your righteousness. Help me to strengthen my desire to always place You first so that my life may be an honor to Your glory, and an example of Your truth and love to my friends, loved ones, and those I may meet. This I ask in the name of Your Son, Jesus Christ. Amen."

Character Test

*"Beloved, do not believe every spirit, but test the
spirits, whether they are of God;
because many false prophets have gone out into the
world." -I John 4:1*

$\mathcal{T}$oday, people sometimes go to great lengths
to get a background check on someone because
they want to have a clear idea of the
individual's character. An employer may want
to know if the person has ever been fired from
a job, and if so, for what reason. They may also
want to know if the person has a criminal
record. Or, another scenario may be one of a
more social nature; a woman may want to
make sure the man she is dating is who he says
he is.

It is sad that we can't always be fully trusting
of one another, but as reality has it, sometimes
people lie, or aren't really the people they
present themselves to be.

Within the Bible, Christ speaks of how we can
better know someone's character by paying
close attention to an individual's actions or
"fruits," for actions speak louder and more
accurately than words.

"Beware of false prophets, who come to you in sheep's clothing, but inwardly they are ravenous wolves. You will know them by their fruits. Do men gather grapes from thorn-bushes or figs from thistles? Even so, every good tree bears good fruit, but a bad tree bears bad fruit. A good tree cannot bear bad fruit, nor can a bad tree bear good fruit. Every tree that does not bear good fruit is cut down and thrown into the fire. Therefore by their fruits you will know them." (Matthew 7:15-20)

Does this mean that good people cannot do wrong (sin), or that evil-hearted people cannot ever do a good deed?

Of course not!

Only God and His Son Jesus Christ is perfect, so there are times even the most staunch believer's have stumbled and fallen. Likewise, even someone as Adolf Hitler who was responsible for the extermination of millions of Jews during the Holocaust had his kind moments as well. However, the larger picture revealed a cold-hearted and hate-dominated individual.

So then, if we all have sinned at one time or another in our life, doesn't that make us all equal?

No! For the difference rests in repentance.
In short, the individual who thirsts after
righteousness will repent of their sin, but
the evil-hearted one will not for they will
not see or care about any wrong in their
evil deed or bitter fruit.

"...But unless you repent, you too will all perish."
(Luke 13:3)

God does not want His children to walk about
the world without wisdom and understanding.
The Bible is full of numerous truths which we
can apply to our lives so that we may live more
abundantly.

 I invite you today, to ask God in to your heart
and life so that these truths may also bless
YOUR life.

Drugs In The Home

𝒜n exasperated mother and father sat down in a counselor's office. Both were at their wits end because, although they did their best to raise their daughter in to a loving, supportive and stable home, with each passing year of her teenaged life, their daughter had become more involved in recreational drugs.

"We've tried everything," stated the mother as she reached for a tissue within her purse. "Even after family counseling and an intervention, then her staying at a rehabilitation center for three months last summer, Jenny is again back to her old ways," the mother continued as she dabbed the tears from her eyes.

Her husband put his hand on her knee, patted it, and added, "It's true. We just don't know what more to do. We love our daughter, and want the best for her, but she doesn't seem to want it for herself. We've tried everything to get her to open her eyes, and while things can change for a little while, she always goes back to the drugs."

The counselor, Mrs. Kelly, had known Jenny's family for a very long time. She knew the type of people they were, and understood their pain and frustration because she had helped other similar families who were going through the same thing. Most were not neglectful parents; the addicts were coming from otherwise stable and loving homes, and this made the situation even more frustrating.

"Growing up in these trying times is not always easy," replied Mrs. Kelly. "As responsible parents we teach our kids one set of morals, but their peers often follow another, and the pressure to fit in can be intense. Add to this the confusing, sexual, and often violent messages and images on TV, in modern music and the entertainment industry, and add to this the easy availability of drugs, and, well, it makes for a very risky breeding ground."

Jenny's parents eyes locked with Mrs. Kelly's as they seemed to cling to her every word.

Mrs. Kelly continued, "It's hard to know why for certain someone falls pray to drugs, and other unhealthy life choices, but the best response we as parents can take while still engaging in other positive actions such as family counseling, etc., is unconditional love."

"We already love, Jenny!" insisted Jenny's dad, "Sometimes, it seems like she doesn't want that love though!"

"That is OK ," said Mrs. Kelly as she smiled

subtly, "Jenny may not want your love right now, but let your actions show her it is there no matter what she may do or say. Love her enough to pray for her daily, even when she may curse you, and let her know that you are there for her when she is ready."

"Yes, but we can't keep living like this!" stated Jenny's dad as he raised up his arms.

Again Mrs. Kelly smiled knowingly, "And you shouldn't have to," she replied, then continued, "Love Jenny enough to continue setting boundaries and consequences. You have other children to think about, as well as your own welfare."

Four years later, Jenny walks in to Mrs. Kelly's office.

"Jenny!" shouted Mrs. Kelly, "You look wonderful! How are you?"

Jenny smiled then sat in the brown worn leather couch. "I am fine," she said, "but I came here to tell you thanks. My parent's told me the advice you gave them years ago, and although I initially thought they were fools for wasting their time, I now see that this was the best thing they could have done for me."

"Oh?" replied Mrs. Kelly as she smiled knowingly.

"Yes, " stated Jenny. "I was not ready and mature enough to quit the drugs. I had to first sink so low that the next step was either up, or down to my grave. My attitude at home got so bad that mom and dad had no choice but to take drastic measures. I hated them for a while, but the recovery center they sent me to really made a difference. Every day for three months we had former addicts share their stories. Being around other recovering addicts also helped me to not feel alone or different, and that it was OK to reach out for help. I also had daily counseling, and a chance to clean out my system of all the garbage that had so polluted it. Even when I was cursing mom and dad, and telling them to stay away, they would still keep in touch, if only to remind me they loved me no matter what. I guess their daily prayers helped because it is quite a miracle how much I have changed! Their consistent love and support made a big difference, and even today, still does!"

Real Life Application: While the above story is fictional, the reality of drugs in our world is real. No longer are drugs solely used by prostitutes, pimps, or the street bum who sits on the dirty sidewalk, but otherwise good and decent families are also being affected. If you know such a family, please consider forwarding this devotional to them.

If you or a loved one is addicted to drugs, please take action, and do not let this monster destroy another family and take another precious life. Alone, it is difficult, but with God at your side, all things are possible!

"Cast your cares on the Lord and he will sustain you..." (Psalms 55:22)

Wrong First Impressions

An elderly woman wrote in to nationally-syndicated columnist, 'Dear Abby,' because she had done something that many of us do: wrongfully judge someone based on first impressions. The woman felt awful because she had terribly pre-judged a male neighbor, simply by how he looked. When he first moved in to the neighborhood, and she saw him all dressed in black; even black nail polish and eye-liner, she marked him as a "devil worshipper." Months later, the long hair he once adorned was completely shaved off, and her next harsh conclusion was that he must now be a radical neo-Nazi "skin-head!" It was only when she took the time to actually get to know her neighbor, that she learned he attended the local university, and was merely dressed in costume for an event the first time she spotted him, and that his long hair was now missing because he regularly donated his fast-growing locks to a charitable association which uses human hair to make wigs for cancer patients who have lost their hair.

The woman felt bad for judging a book by its cover, and wrote in to warn others of doing the same.

How thankful we should be that God does not

judge us the way mankind often does; only by what is seen on the outside. Our Heavenly Father is more concerned about what's going on in the inside; within our hearts and minds, as it is these which control our actions and what comes out of our mouths.

Do you love God and His Son, Jesus Christ? Do you treat others as you yourself wish to be treated?

If yes, you do well, but if not, it is never too late to take that first positive step toward salvation.

Reach out your hand whether it is yellow, black or white for God is the 'Master Painter' who created all these beautiful colors of the spectrum!

Extend out those fingers regardless if they have long or short nails; are adorned with color, or are au natural, for God wants your love, not your nail polish, fashions trends, hair styles, or make-up techniques.

Prayer: "Dear God, please forgive me if I have been shallow, and in my criticism of others, I may have missed rich opportunities to share your truth, or to know someone wonderful. I ask You, God, to help me see others as You do; to give me the same patience You have given me, and to allow all I do and say to be a

walking testimony of Your merciful love. This
I ask in the name of Your Son, Jesus Christ.
Amen."

A Story of True Thanks

"In every thing give thanks: for this is the will of
God in Christ Jesus concerning you."
- 1 Thessalonians 5:18

℣t was Private Smith's third

thanksgiving away from home. The first, he
spent in South Korea. His day began with
latrine duty, and ended with a cold turkey
sandwich and eight hours of guard duty.
The twenty year old Smith's second
Thanksgiving away from loved ones
occurred in the tepid desert near Egypt.
This time, the mess-hall was able to serve a
hot three-course turkey dinner, but due to a
sudden terrible sandstorm, all the food was
sadly ruined, and soldiers were sent on
their way with a peanut butter and jelly
sandwich and pat on the back.

"This year it better be different!" grumbled the
young private as he sat on his cot cleaning his
riffle…in Baghdad. He turned to a fellow
solider, his good buddy, Private Handale, and
quietly said, "I miss those family
Thanksgivings at home where mom would fix
the finest spread north of the Mississippi!
After dinner, dad would gather us around and

read the story of the first Thanksgiving. Mom would then cuddle up close to him and read from the Bible; verses on thankfulness."

The brown-haired private took a deep breath, and said, "What do I have to be thankful for now? Nothing! "

Just then, an awful screeching sound, then earth-shattering explosion broke the somber silence.

Two weeks later…

An unfamiliar female voice quietly stated, *"Give thanks to the Lord, for he is good; his love endures forever." (Psalm 107:1)* Private Smith heard the voice, but he couldn't see anyone in the room.

"Wait a minute!" he thought. "Where am I?"

"Doctor!" shouted the female voice. "Come quick! He appears to be coming out his coma!"

"Coma?" thought Private Smith. "Are they talking about me?"

Just then, the young Smith opened his eyes,

and whispered to the young lady in white who was now peering down excitedly at him, "Was that a Bible verse?"
"Why yes!" the blonde-haired nurse replied.

Suddenly, there were bright lights shining in his eyes, and the feel of cold metal on his chest.

"Heart and lungs are good. "Blood pressure normal," said the doctor matter-of-factly. He continued, "How do you feel, son? Do remember anything?"

Private Smith whispered his name, rank and serial number, while the doctor chuckled. Setting his stethoscope down, he then turned to the nurse and replied, "You've just witnessed a miracle, my dear. Take good care of him."

With that, he walked away to attend to his other many patients.

Private Smith again turned to the nurse, "Why did you say that Bible verse to me?"

She smiled and replied, "Because today is Thanksgiving, and after what you have been through, surely you would be thankful!"

The young private looked puzzled. "Been through?"

"Oh my, I thought you knew," the nurse kindly said as she grabbed the young man's hand. "You have been in a coma for two weeks. You were very seriously injured and we weren't sure you would make it. From what I understand, you saved your friend, Private Handale's life, by covering his body with yours. You are a hero, you know, and you'll receive a purple heart for your bravery and sacrifice."

"Sacrifice?" asked Private Smith quietly.

"There's something more," replied the nurse, "You lost your leg in the explosion."

The young solider reached down and felt the area where his right leg used to be, and then there were a few moments of silence…which broke in to odd snickering.

"Why are you laughing?" asked the confused nurse.

Private Smith went on to explain, "For quite a while now I have found it very difficult to be thankful on Thanksgiving, and maybe even other days as well. I guess that is because I was trying to be glad for the wrong things; things I thought were important, but really aren't, at least not in the greater scheme of things. Yes, I lost my leg, but I gained something even more precious; my life! I am also so very thankful that my best friend, Private Handale, is alive for he has been such a help and blessing to me for these last three years. If the number of deaths from that attack was as great as you say, then how ungrateful it would be for me to complain about one silly missing leg, while other families are grieving their losses. No, I am not sad, but thankful, grateful and glad for what I have!"

Just then, the doctor walked in the room to hand deliver a telegram. "It's from your family. Nurse, please read this to him"

The blonde-haired nurse cleared her throat, and read the contents of the note:

"Dear son, we are overjoyed beyond words to hear of your miraculous recovery! We wish we could be there with you. This is the best Thanksgiving, for we are so very thankful to God for the simple gift of life! We love you so much, and we are anxious to see you soon! Praise God!"

With tears now streaming from his eyes, the young private Smith replied to his family as if they were standing there beside him. "And this is MY best thanksgiving too!"

Fear Of Death

"O death, where is your sting? O grave, where is your victory?" -1 Corinthians 15:55

I am not typically a fearful person, but I must admit that after my brother's unexpected death last year I began to have obsessive thoughts concerning possibly again losing someone near and dear to me. Not only did Nick's sudden demise make me see just how fragile life is, but I quickly also learned that no matter how we may plan and prepare, there is no avoiding the fact we all will one day die.

I came to this conclusion after months of pondering various "what-if" scenarios concerning my husband, adult-aged children, siblings and parents. Meaning, I would ask myself, "What if _____ suddenly died? What would I do?" I also went ahead and had my end of life and 'upon my death' wishes put in writing.

Thankfully, my fear subsided when, after much ado, there was no more to be done. And so, I went back to simply ...living.

A lot of people fear death, and while I cannot

honestly say that at age forty-five I am anxiously looking forward to it, I do accept it's inevitability. And because I believe what the Bible says about the gift of salvation and eternal life to those who love God and His Son, Jesus Christ, death, for me, is not final, but is merely a passageway to another plane of existence. ("That if you confess with your mouth, "Jesus is Lord," and believe in your heart that God raised him from the dead, you will be saved." -Romans 10:9) As someone once said, "We are not flesh and blood beings who have a spiritual mission, but rather, we are spiritual beings on a flesh and blood mission."

That mission, my friend, is to glorify God by how we live our life, and to preach God's good news to everyone who has an ear to listen.

If you fear death, then won't you replace worry and doubt with the peace and comfort that can only come from a relationship with your Creator?

Dangerous Beliefs

𝒯here is a dangerous theory going around which some people are being led astray by. The theory proclaims that everything which occurs is a sole result of predestination. In lay-mans terms, predestination means that something was planned by God. According to this viewpoint, this even means that when a child is abducted, raped, tortured and murdered, God planned it. It also means God was fully responsible for the Holocaust, the deaths of thousands when the terrorists forced airplanes to crash in to the twin towers in New York City on 9-11, and other horrendous evil acts. The theory also affirms that we reach for certain foods and drinks because, you guessed it, this is our destiny!

While the Bible does relay that God has utilized predestination when He deemed fit, Scriptures also reveal the reality of man's ability to freely think and act of his own will.

"What man is he that feareth the LORD? him shall he teach in the way that he shall choose."
                    -Psalm 25:12

"For that they hated knowledge, and did not choose the fear of the LORD.."
-Proverbs 1:29

"Envy thou not the oppressor, and choose none of his ways."-Proverbs 3:31

To accept only half the truth (predestination) while turning our back on another truth (free-will), is still not the whole truth.

Man-made theories which come about as a result of twisting Scripture, or picking out convenient bits and pieces, is deceptive, and has the ability to lead people astray by changing the character of God, and taking responsibility off man, and placing all blame for all things on God. For example, such a theory supports that when someone abuses drugs or alcohol, or commit's a crime, it is not their fault, but God's, since, after all, it was their presumed God-inspired destiny. Thus so, God is made to look like a moronic twit by those who hold dear to this man-made theory because it means that God even predestined Lucifer, the former angel of light whom we now know as satan, to desire to be higher than the one true God. Again God is made to appear as a silly idiot by warning Adam and Eve to not eat of a certain tree in the garden, yet, according to this inaccurate theory, the Lord predestined them to disobey Him. The deceptive doctrine also supports that Christ did not die for ALL men as the Scriptures proclaim, but only those on the presumed predestined list. Once again, God is then made to look like an incompetent ninny who in one breath tells His disciples to go and preach His word to the nations so that all men may come to know His glory, yet, He presumably foolishly predestines only certain people to believe! If this is the case, then why bother evangelizing?

My dear friend, the Bible warns us that in the last days there will be deceivers. (*"For the time will come when they will not endure sound doctrine; but wanting to have their ears tickled, they will accumulate for themselves teachers in accordance to their own desires and will turn away their ears from the truth, and will turn aside to myths."* - II Timothy 4:3-4)

Just as we need to be careful of unscrupulous solicitors who knock on our door, or try to get credit card information on the phone for their own wicked purposes, likewise, we need to be aware of belief systems which push us father from the truth of God's word, as opposed to closer.

If you are dabbling in the negative occult, such as dealing with psychics and mediums, or you have been holding on to beliefs that are not fully steeped in God's truth (the Bible), won't you please consider releasing their grip within your life?

Prayer: Heavenly Father, I have allowed
myself to be involved in things that have been
a dishonor to You. I am sorry, God, and I ask
You to forgive me and help me start anew.
This I ask in the name of Your Son, Jesus
Christ. Amen.

A True Story of Healing

"But Jesus beheld them, and said unto them, With men this is impossible; but with God all things are possible." -Matthew 19:26

𝒯he below is a true story as revealed to me by a reader who wrote to share a miraculous story with me. With her permission, this is how she described the physical healing of her daughter, Barbara:

She [Barbara] was born with brain damage from the forceps. She never spoke a word that could be understood. At eight years old, I took her to a healing service. During communion, the Pastor told me that brain cells were being healed on this cute little red head. On the way down from communion, she looked at me, and as plain as day said "Mommy, why are you crying like that?" An instant miracle! Today she is 37 and still has perfect speech."

When a skeptic hears such a wondrous story, they may shake their head, roll their eyes and say, "Oh, that is just coincidence! I know the Bible speaks of presumed miracles, but that was a very long time ago."

Yes, the Scriptures do reveal many signs and

wonders, but let us not forget that Christ
himself was a miracle! From the immaculate
conception of his birth, to his resurrection after
his death on the cross, and everything which
occurred in between, miraculous, would
certainly be an appropriate word to define
Jesus' life here on earth. However, there were
skeptics then, and they still exist now.

Why is it so hard for some people to accept the
reality of miraculous events?

I suppose one can compare the denial with
same type of blindness that causes many of us
to turn our backs on our own shortcomings.
We may think we are upstanding citizens, but
the reality may be that we are selfish,
thoughtless and mean-spirited. For such
individuals, admitting they are less than
perfect is almost inconceivable, and it seems
easier to continue on in their unrighteous
ways, than to change what needs fixing.

My dear friend, I have experienced miracles
within my own life, so I know they are real. So
too do I know that God is real. Hearing such
stories of healings and various dramatic life
transformations does not surprise me because I
know that with God, all things are possible!

What about you?

Are you ready to experience great signs and

wonders within your own life?

Prayer: "Dear God, I want to know You, and want to know what is and isn't real, but I am afraid. However, I am willing to set my fear and skepticism aside so that I can give You (and myself!) a fair chance. I know I have made a lot of mistakes in my life which have caused myself and others a great deal of pain, but I am now ready to have You wash me clean of my sins so that I may start anew as Your child. Please give me new eyes to see with so I won't be so negative and critical, and help my hard heart to soften. This I ask in the name of Your Son, Jesus Christ. Amen."

Do The Right Thing!

*S*ometimes I wonder if the fear of being "politically-correct" or not intruding on an individual's "diversity" may be preventing the truth of God's word, the Bible, from being revealed to the masses.

Perhaps we don't want to step on anyone's toes or risk offending someone by sharing with them information God clearly says they need to hear. (*"Therefore go and make disciples of all nations, baptizing them in the name of the Father and of the Son and of the Holy Spirit..." -Matthew 28:19*)

My dear friend, if we do not want God to be ashamed to call us His children, then likewise, we should not be ashamed of Him and His word. It is not for us to judge His message as presented in the Scriptures, but to simply do as He has asked, for we are not here to please man, but God. (*"On the contrary, we speak as men approved by God to be entrusted with the gospel. We are not trying to please men but God, who tests our hearts." - 1 Thessalonians 2:4*)

I am reminded of a period in time when many people said nothing about racism and prejudice due to fear of speaking out, and standing up for what was right. The result of this inactivity was that evil was allowed to continue on.

When you care about someone, you warn them if they are about to stumble off a cliff. And, if you see an individual about to drink poison which he thinks is lemonade, you likewise make certain they know that sipping the beverage will lead to their sickness and demise.

If this is the case, then why, dear friend, are we often fearful and hesitant to share the truth of God's word with a world that so desperately needs to hear it?

Some people will accept God's word, and others will reject it. Doing so may cause us to make friends, or enemies. However, truth is truth, and it is God's business, not our own, for as the Scriptures affirm, *"For we do not preach ourselves, but Jesus Christ as Lord, and ourselves as your servants for Jesus' sake."* -2 Corinthians 4:5

Taking a stand for the truth, and doing what is right is not always easy. In fact, in this day and age, it can be quite difficult at times because what God has to say on a given subject may not always match with our current society's view. For example, man may say that having a sexual relationship outside of marriage is not a big deal, but God's word declares adultery as sin. (*"Marriage should be honored by all, and the marriage bed kept pure, for God will judge the adulterer and all the sexually immoral."* *-Hebrews 13:4*) Likewise, our friends may tell us its acceptable to lie, cheat and steal, but is this really what God would have us do?

No, it is not always easy to do the right thing, but the rewards which come as a result are more than well worth it!

What's It Going To Take?

"And The Lord said to Moses, "How long will this people despise Me? And how long will they not believe in Me, in spite of all the signs which I have wrought among them?" (Numbers 14:11)

Some people just don't seem to get it. Or maybe they don't even care, or feel it necessary to think about things within the spiritual realm as God and the afterlife. They live in the here and now; only wanting to deal with what is before them at the moment. Those individuals who believe and have experienced the reality of God in their life may reveal profound personal transformations and other signs and wonders which followed their faith in God, and yet, as the above Bible verse reveals, in spite of the signs, those they have spoke with still will not believe.

Sadly, many people exist in this world totally oblivious to God. And as such, I must ask myself, "What's it going to take for them to open their blind eyes, deaf ears and hard hearts?" Will someone close to them have to die before they raise their own questions on life after death? Does sickness or disease have to befall them before they humble themselves enough to cry out to the Lord? Must their own life be endangered before they shout, "Help

me, God!" Worse yet, what if they put off God
until it is too late?

Again, I ask, what's it going to take?

In essence, God has prepared an awesome feast
for us all, but His invitation to partake of it is
continually ignored.

> "*And Jesus answered and spake unto them
> again by parables, and said, The kingdom of
> heaven is like unto a certain king, which made a
> marriage for his son, And sent forth his servants
> to call them that were bidden to the wedding:
> and they would not come.*" (Matthew 22:1)

What about you?

What's it going to take for you to take
notice of the One who has been calling and
reaching out to you?

Prayer: "Dear God, I have hid from You
long enough. I have lived according to my
own devices, and they have failed
miserably. I am ready to take hold of Your
hand now, God, and to start anew. Come
in to my life, dear Lord, and soften my
heart with Your love. This I ask in the
name of Your Son, Jesus Christ. Amen."

What Is Born Again?

While visiting my mother recently, it was a particularly pleasant day, so we partook of the fresh air and sunshine by pouring ourselves a cool beverage and pulling out two comfortable chairs. As we sat and chatted, I noticed a spry elderly woman who seemed lost. I called out, and ushered her over. She must have felt safe and comfortable in our presence as talk of directions quickly began to turn in to diverse social chatter. Upon hearing that she was a long-time Catholic who had recently lost her son, and was having a very difficult time dealing with her overwhelming feelings of grief, I attempted to offer her some friendly advice which I found helpful in coming to terms with the loss of my brother who had passed away shortly before. "What really helped 'me' was my faith," I said quietly.

Immediately, the conversation, and the look upon her face changed. "Don't tell me you are one of those 'born-agains,'" she quipped. Upon nodding, I was then issued a stern rebuke. "I guess *those people* weren't born the first time!" she said snippily as she looked at my mother who sat there dumbfounded, most likely fearful of what retort could come out of my own mouth. Despite the fact hundreds of words spun around my head; all of them which could have easily formed a full-length Bible study, I decided it would be best to say nothing, as the Scriptures relay there is a time and place for all things.

We spoke a bit longer, and when she left, I smiled and waved good-bye.

Had I taken a different approach to this woman's jabbing comment against my faith, knowing full-well she was in the throws of mourning, I would not have given her what she needed right then and there. In other words, her grief was more important than my feelings of insult. Besides, I hoped that my subdued response would be more effective than any sharp retort of my own, for there are times when actions speak louder than words. And so, I left it in God's hands, trusting Him to one day inform her what her own love of God and His word affirms.

Unfortunately, this is not the first time I have heard people mock or attack the concept of being "born-again," not seeming to know that the term is derived from the Bible itself (John 3:1-5):

> *"Now there was a Pharisee named Nicodemus, a leader of the Jews. He came to Jesus by night and said to him, "Rabbi, we know that you are a teacher who has come from God; for no one can do these signs that you do apart from the*

presence of God."
Jesus answered him, "Very truly, I tell you, no
one can see the kingdom of God without being
born again.* *" Nicodemus said to him, "How*
can anyone be born after having grown old?
Can one enter a second time into the mother's
womb and be born?" Jesus answered, "Very
truly, I tell you, no one can enter the kingdom of
God without being born of water and Spirit."
-John 3:1-5

As the above Scriptures reveal, obviously
Christ was not using the term "born again" in a
literal sense, but rather, in a figurative sense;
the concept that it is available for us to be new
creations as we are washed clean and freed
from a sinful past, and able to begin a new life
in Christ by way of the Holy Spirit.

"But my parents had me baptized as a baby,"
you may say, "Isn't that enough to be saved?"

That's just it. Your 'parents' decided for you at
a time in your life when you could not speak or
decide on your own. However, you are no
longer a child, but now an adult in your own
right who has his/her own mind. Not
everyone remains in the faith to which they
were born. Just as Catholics regard what they
refer to as "confirmation" as "a sacrament of
initiation into the Christian life," (source:
www.Catholic.com), so too does Christ's
mandate to be "born again" support this same

concept of spiritual rebirth and transformation.

Various denominations of Christianity may refer to the above act in differing terms, but whether they specifically describe themselves as such (born again) or not, our Heavenly Father, God, is more concerned with what rests in our heart, than over what word we use to define our spiritual walk with Him.

Besides, we are not "saved" by water, but by the grace of God which is bestowed on all who adhere to the truth set forth in Romans 10:9-10 of the Bible:

"That if you confess with your mouth, "Jesus is Lord," and believe in your heart that God raised him from the dead, you will be saved."

Despite the fact Christ clearly tells us in the Bible that we must be born again, somewhere along the line this act has picked up a negative connotation. Whether it is satan at work, or our own lack of knowledge, as the old saying goes, "Ignorance is not bliss."

"Dear God, there have been times in my life that I have ridiculed, even hated, those things which I have not fully understood. On occasion, I have been rude, thoughtless and mean-spirited. Indeed, I have sinned much, but I am now ready and willing to set my past aside, and to be transformed according to what is good and pleasing in Your sight. I humbly place my heart before you, God, as an open vessel. Help me to fill it, God, with Your truth, love and light. This I ask in the name of Your Son, Jesus Christ. Amen."

Why I Am I Born Again

"Jesus answered him, "Very truly, I tell you, no one can see the kingdom of God without being born again." -John 3:1-5

In a previous Daily Wisdom I wrote on what it means to be "born again." I chose that topic because there seemed to a definite lack of understanding, even amongst fellow Believers, as to what the term meant, and the fact Christ calls us to be born again in the Bible.

In keeping with similar subject matter, I would like to take this topic one step further, and share with you why I became born again.

While I was raised believing in God, even attending private faith-based elementary and secondary schooling, and can't recall a time in my life I didn't believe in God and His Son, Jesus Christ, the denomination my parents chose for me at birth was no longer a good fit for me as a (young) adult. While I respected their right to chose as they deemed suitable, and am very thankful for the spiritual foundation they had provided me, my personal spiritual path took me on a journey of my own. However, it was not leaving one denomination and entering in to another which made me born-again, but rather, what was occurring deeply within my own heart.

My thirst for spiritual truth was causing me to want to reach higher and look deeper. I wanted to be a better person; to be more pleasing in God's sight. While I don't recall the exact moment or actual words spoken, the basic sentiment I am trying to convey is that I made a conscious decision to now make Christ number one in my life. This would require change and action.

Everything was going better than wonderfully, and then, several years later, and by my own wrongful choices, began to take a severe nose-dive. I speak in detail about what was then my drug and alcohol dabbling period in my book, *"Ecstatic Living/Ecstatic Loving: A marriage manual and life-guide."* In brief, when I moved by myself to the other side of the country, I got caught up in an unhealthy and fast-paced life-style I was not prepared to deal with, and to which nearly killed me. Upon hitting rock bottom, I, thankfully, had enough wits about me to realize the need for a serious transformation because it finally sunk in that I was living the life of a hypocrite; attempting to mix godliness with ungodliness. As such, I needed to transform and recommit, and that is exactly what I did.

I know people who experienced this rebirth once in their life, and I also am familiar with individuals who have similar experience to my own, and for one reason or another, (slow learners?), have more than one major transformation event. My own reason for being born again was that I quite simply needed it. I didn't like the life choices I was making, who I was becoming, and where I was heading. Life seemed so shallow, and I wanted to not only find its meaning, but to live the life we are called here to live. Long ago, God gave me a glimpse of the bigger picture, and from then on, I wanted more. I wanted to 'be' more.

If you want more too, I encourage you to call out to God today, and be reborn in your spirit, so that you may live that awesome life God has in store for you!

Hurtful Gossip

I hate to say it but it seems some of my family relations love to gossip.

Desiring to know how various family relations are doing, and wanting to know what's going on in their life is one thing, but when gossip hurts, then it is time to reevaluate if our wish to "be informed" is being used for good, or something quite the opposite.

Sometimes a relation will say to me, "Oh, you wouldn't believe what _____ said about you!" Years ago, I would have taken that bait, allowed the comments to hurt me, and then strain my relationship with the other party, but I have learned that there are so many other more important things in life to concern ourselves with than to worry about what this or that person thinks of me. The way I see it is, I answer to God, and my self. If others have a problem with that, so be it, for within this lifetime, we will never be able to please all people all of the time. There will always be someone who doesn't care for our style of dress, the way we comb our hair, or the way we react in any given situation. However, as long as we are pleasing God, then He, not aunt Helen or cousin Henry, is our standard.

Today, when someone says the above, my response is now, "If it's something negative about me, or something that will upset me, I'd rather not hear it."

What about you and your dealings with others? If Jesus were listening in on your conversations, would you feel proud or ashamed over the contents of your speech? If the Son of God were standing beside you, would your actions be different?

In the Bible we are told, *"Be not deceived; God is not mocked: for whatsoever a man sows, that he also reap." -Galatians 6:7*

What this basically means is that if we sow seeds of discord, this is what will return to us, for would it be right for man to sow hate, and hope to gain love in return?

Of course not!

Prayer: "Dear God, please help me to see areas in my life that may need improvement, for it is my heart's desire to be pleasing to You. Show me how I can mend any wounds I have opened, and that my presence in the lives of others can be as a blessing, not a curse. I am sorry if I have offended You, and others, God, but I am now ready to set the past behind me, and to begin as a new creation. Help me to love others, as You love me. This I ask in the name of Your Son, Jesus Christ. Amen."

A Higher Standard

A long time ago, when my children were still very young, I made the decision to stop only using the "good dishes" when company was here or it was some holiday. After all, wasn't our family precious enough all by itself? Why not treat every day as a special occasion?

Now, many years later, I still carry this practice with me, but I now regard it as more of a life philosophy; the concept of trying to always give what is most important in the life the best of me. What IS most important is God, then family.

Doing this has not always been easy as it sometimes required a bit of sacrifice, but the rewards, both earthly and spiritual, have been nothing short of astounding! My relationship with God has strengthened and grown as a result of placing God in the number one spot He deserves, and the sense of unity and love present within our family brings a sense of peace and joy to my heart because I know that while I have not been the perfect parent, I have given the role my genuine best effort.

I wonder what the world would be like if everyone put God and family first. Divorce rates, crime, and various forms of immorality would go down, and people would simply be happier because they would be lovingly nurtured in a family foundation of love and support.

My dear friends, if this sounds like a utopian idea, rest assured, it is not. In fact, it is the way God desires us to live, as the Scriptures clearly state, "   "

Today, won't you consider raising the standard of your life so that it may be all that it could be? After all, aren't YOU worth it?

Prayer: "Heavenly Father, I desire to know You, and to find out what it is you require of me, and my life. I come before you kneeling because I am a sinner. I ask for You to wash me clean of my past transgressions so that I may become a new creation whose heart's desire is only to do what is good and right in Your sight. I thank you for giving me the strength and courage to let my actions speak louder than words so that I may never be ashamed of Your powerful presence within me. This I humbly ask in the name of Your Son, Jesus Christ. Amen.

Discovered

I recently "discovered" a profound musical talent named Andrea Bocelli. As reality has it, Mr. Bocelli, an Italian born tenor who is said to have the voice of an angel, has been around for many years, and I don't know how his beautiful voice could have escaped my ears for so long, but, well, such was my loss!

In my admitted ignorance, I called my mother to tell her about Andrea, knowing how she appreciates her own Italian heritage, as well as good classical music. However, much to my chagrin, when I called mom, she replied, "Oh! Of course I know who he is! I have loved his music for years!"

"You have?" I said as I felt my own excitement quickly drain from me.

Mom then went on to list a few of her favorite Bocelli songs; even going so far as to inform me of several CD's of his she now owns, which is quite shocking to me since my seventy-five year old mother has never even warmly embraced such modern technology as a personal computer or DVD player.

After I hung up the phone and allowed all of this new information to digest, I couldn't help but also relate the issue to those individuals who walk the earth and go about their daily lives totally oblivious to God. Just as I missed out on this musical experience; proudly thinking I was "in the know," how many people are missing out on their very salvation because they think they know everything there is to know?

Prayer: "Heavenly Father, please forgive me for ignoring your Divine presence. I want to know You and Your will for my life. Come in to my heart, dear God, and let me know the depth of your love. This I ask in the name of Your Son, Jesus Christ. Amen."

Saved At Sea

𝒜 wealthy family decided to rent a yacht for their upcoming vacation. The father had no experience in sailing, but as everything in life seemed to come easy to him, he boasted that this too should be no problem.

The family loaded everything they needed for their world-wide cruise; clothes for every occasion, make-up, fancy jewelry and the finest perfumes, since, one never knows what kings, queens or heads of state may greet them at each port.

Living in such opulence was nothing new to the Van Dyke family. Both parents were raised with the proverbial silver spoons in their mouths; attended to by nannies, butlers and grounds-keepers, and they raised their two children in the same lap of luxury.

What should have been a pleasure cruise began to slowly turn in to a nightmare after only a few days at sea. The radio died, but always expecting the best, Mr. Van Dyke ignored the breaking of this necessary communication which would have also allowed him to hear of the impending storm they were heading right in to.

Before long, the white yacht was being rocked to and fro by massive waves, and pummeled by bullets of hard rain.

"Not to worry," said Mr. Van Dyke calmly. "Let's just tie down our valuables as we wouldn't want to lose anything important!"

Mrs. Van Dyke took a silk sash from her bathrobe, wrapped it around her large ivory jewelry box, then tied the box to the post of her bed in hopes no ring, necklace or bangle would shift out of place. Likewise, the Van Dyke children, Martha and Ben, gathered up all their toys and electronic game equipment, and placed them in a wooden chest. "Wouldn't want anything to happen to my Xbot!" exclaimed ten year old Ben.

Just as Mr. Van Dyke was pondering what valuable he should be most concerned with, a towering wall of water smacked their vessel so hard, the yacht fell to its side. Immediately, the ship began taking on water, and there was nothing anyone could do to stop it. "We need to get off the boat! It's going to sink!" yelled Mr. Van Dyke. In the blink of an eye another massive wave came and washed the entire family into the dark waters of the raging sea. As they fought to stay afloat, Mr. And Mrs. Van Dyke frantically tried to get to Martha and Ben who not only did not know how to swim, but who also were not wearing life-jackets.

The look of terror was upon the faces of the entire family. For the first time in his life, Mr. Van Dyke, the typically over-confident and self-centered business executive was now helpless and unsure what next to do. As Martha and Ben's tiny bodies slipped under the turbulent water, Mr. Van Dyke cried out a blood-curdling scream of, "Dear God! Please!" Seeing her children being swallowed up by the waves, Mrs. Van Dyke dove under the water to where her little ones were, and pushed them back to the surface. Suddenly, Mr. Van Dyke noticed something floating; a plank of wood from the children's toy box. "Grab tight to the plank!" He shouted. "Don't let go!"

While the sea began to slowly calm, all around the family was still water, and all that was left of their yacht was the tip of it which had yet to be swallowed up.

Martha began to cry. "I don't want to die, Mommy!"

"I don't want to die either, dear," replied Mrs. Van Dyke as every muscle in her body ached from treading water so long.

Both the Van Dyke's knew the situation was very grave, and that there was a chance their family would not come out of this alive.

"I would like us to pray," said Mr. Van Dyke as he too struggled to stay afloat.

"But we have never prayed before, Daddy," whimpered Ben as his tiny body shivered from the cool waters.

"I know we haven't, and that was a terrible mistake I made," said Mr. Van Dyke. "I guess I was so busy with other things I thought were important, but now I can see they really weren't."

"What your father is trying to say, dear, is, all that is important is you!" cried out Mrs. Van Dyke as she began to flounder in the sea; her arms beginning to give out.

"Your mother is right. It was a big mistake, and I hope you…and God…will forgive me," replied Mr. Van Dyke as he accidentally swallowed a gulp of salty sea water; his arms also so weary from treading the thick waters. He continued, "Martha and Ben, promise me that no matter what happens, you will not let go of the plank. Also promise me that in your life as you grow older, you will put God first, and family second."

"We will, Dad. We promise," said Martha and Ben in unison as their little fists turned red from holding on to the plank so tightly.

"Alright then. Let us pray," said Mr. Van Dyke as he lead his family in prayer for the first time.

[Hours later]

"Mr. Van Dyke? Can you hear me yet, Sir?" whispered the voice of a woman clad in white.

Slowly, his eyes opened, and while confused of his whereabouts, Mr. Van Dyke's first thought went to his wife and children.

"It's OK, Sir. Your family is safe and all on dry land here in the Coast Guard hospital," replied the nurse assuredly. "Your rescuers were able to salvage a few things from the yacht, and here is one of them I thought you might like."

The nurse held Mrs. Van Dykes ivory jewelry box.

Mr. Van Dyke took it in his weak hands, and upon opening it, saw that it was still intact. Looking at the nurse he said, "You know, I paid millions of dollars for the contents of this box."

Upon closing the lid, he replied, "Give this to the hospital. I don't need it. I already have everything truly valuable I need."

Spiritual Application: The above story is purely fictional, yet for many of us, it is reality that a relationship with God is pushed to the back burner of our life, and like Mr. Van Dyke, replaced with other things which seem important, but really aren't. The Van Dykes realized this in time, and thankfully, had a second chance to begin anew, but how many people go to their grave without even considering God and their spiritual welfare?

My dear friends, do not put off 'till tomorrow what you can do today. It is never too late to start anew!

True Beauty

"...beauty is vain: but a woman that feareth the Lord, she shall be praised."
                              -Proverbs 31:30

Ten years ago, a summer daytrip to the beach caused me to notice all the "sun worshippers" who lay basking in our arid Florida heat in an attempt to, what they most-likely believed, was to beautify their appearance with a bronze-hue. As I temporarily joined the sun-bunny crowd for the day, my reason being that I needed to watch my then younger children as they played in the refreshing surf, I began to consider the damaging affects of the sun. I couldn't help but wonder if we are so vain about our outer beauty that we are willing to endure the appearance of premature aging, denser and tougher skin texture, and the risk of skin cancer?

How glad I am that God does not care much about how our outer shells look, for our physical body is a non-permanent casing and not a true reflection of who we truly are. Just as you cannot judge a book by its cover, so too is the real story about who we are inside our hearts, minds and characters.

Sure, it's nice to like what we see when we look in the mirror, but sometimes we all need a reminder that it is more important to be pleasing in God's sight.

Prayer: "Heavenly Father, please help me to find the beauty inside myself. Wash me clean with your merciful grace, and provide in me a pure heart: one that is a true reflection of your love. This I ask in the name of Your son, Jesus Christ. Amen."

Dangerous Internet?

"Keep sound wisdom and discretion…Then you will walk safely in your way." -Proverbs 3:21-23

*O*ur most profound recent technological advance, in my view, is the Internet, because it not only allows us to have a vast supply of knowledge at our fingertips, but it has also transformed how people communicate.

Some men and women who would never even think of striking up a very close friendship with a member of the opposite sex due to it's possible temptations, may not think twice over engaging in daily personal chats and letters with a cyber acquaintance.

While the Internet can be an awesome research tool, just as we exercise caution in real life, it would be wise to also apply discretion when using the Internet. Like any large city, the Internet contains certain undesirable communities which are best avoided. Roam in to one of these areas, whether by accident or sheer curiosity, and you may find yourself exposed to words and behaviors which test and tempt moral character.

Just as you would avoid a high crime area of

town, why permit yourself to drift in to areas on the World Wide Web which could jeopardize your spiritual walk?

The same is true with who we associate with on the Internet. Due to the fact we have no way to truly know who we are communicating with, unscrupulous individuals have been known to be deceptive about their age, marital status, career and motives. I am sure we have all heard the stories of husbands and wives who become so close to someone they have met on the Internet, that they end up abandoning their marriage, and emotionally devastating their family's.

Once again, such heartbreaks can be prevented if we are wise enough to see possible temptation before we enter these danger zones. If you wouldn't tell your life story to a stranger on the street, why do it to someone you don't know on the Internet? If you wouldn't pursue a warm and fuzzy friendship with someone you are physically attracted to face to face, then why think there is less threat posed by a similar situation in the cyber realm?

Friendship is a beautiful thing, but let us not place the importance of our desire to relate to another human being, before godly discretion.

Prayer: "Heavenly Father, help me to see those things in my life which may be displeasing to You. Give me the strength to walk away from temptation, and break my ties to sin. This I humbly ask in the name of Your Son, Jesus Christ. Amen."

Feeling Frail?

"He was despised and rejected by men, a man of sorrows, and familiar with suffering. Like one from whom men hide their faces, he was despised and we esteemed him not. Surely, he took up our infirmities and carried our sorrows, yet we considered him stricken by God, smitten by him, and afflicted. But he was pierced for our transgressions, he was crushed for our iniquities; the punishment that brought us peace was upon him, and by his wounds we are healed." - Isaiah 53:3-5

*H*appiness and sadness are emotions we all face in life. We rejoice over our successes and share these happy moments freely with others, but what do we do with our miseries, disappointments, fears, regrets, and worries? Happiness is an easy thing to share, but sadness, is usually a dark and lonely road, for, it is during these periods our weaknesses and vulnerabilities are shown.

"My guilt has overwhelmed me like a burden too heavy to bear." - Psalm 38:4

Why are we so frightened to admit we are human, that we cannot carry all the weight of the world, and that there will be moments our knees buckle from too heavy a load?

It is not God's intent for His children to deal with their burdens alone.

In the Bible, we are instructed, "*Cast your cares on the Lord and he will sustain you...*" (Psalms 55:22). Although we may sometimes be weak due to our fleshly nature, God is strong and can offer comfort. It is also not God's will to let those individuals who are struggling with sorrow handle their troubles alone, but instead, we are wisely told to, "*Love your neighbor as yourself.*" (Galatians 5:14)

Jesus Christ, the Son of God, experienced suffering and sorrow while on earth. As such, we do not have to dwell on our sorrows alone, but how comforting to know that we can turn them over to One who truly understands, and can ease our pains like none other!

Won't you place His healing balm of love upon your wounds, and receive His gift of salvation?

Prayer: "God, I know you love me as a Father. I am hurting, and I need you to take me in to your care. I invite you in to my heart and life so that I may not walk this path alone. Amen."

The Choice Is Yours

I have never understood how people can complain about how unsatisfying their life is, yet they do nothing to improve it.

"Drugs have really messed me up!" says one young woman. "I hate this job; it's been the same thing day in and day out for ten years!" shouts a middle-aged father. "Nothing in my life seems to go the way I want. I feel like such a failure," replies a single mother.

How easy it is to whine and complain, perhaps even blame our discontentment on others, fate, or God's presumed abandonment. The truth of the matter is that it is quite often by our own inactivity that the same frustrations and displeasures we experienced yesterday, will still be with us today, tomorrow and for as long as we do nothing to create positive change.

While I have been happily married for twenty-one years, there was a time in my younger days when the course my life was going on began to slowly take a detour. The change was so subtle that I could not see the gradual downward spiral which was instigated by a period of dabbling in recreational drugs and alcohol. The substances began to change my personality, and taint my sense of right and wrong.

While it took some time for me to come to this point, I thankfully began to see that my current choices were pulling me farther from my family, true friends, God, and my dreams of the future.

All it took for me was a decision. I didn't like who I had become, and where my life was going, so I simply and immediately began to act upon that decision. I was dirty though. My mind, body and spirit was polluted and ill from ungodly living. As such, I recommitted my life to Christ, asking for His merciful forgiveness and cleansing. I admitted my weakness to God, and asked for His wisdom and strength. "Help me, God, to see and only follow that which is good, right and true according to Your word and will," I prayed.

In the Bible, we are told that believing is ACTION. (*"So with faith; if it does not lead to action, it is in itself a lifeless thing." -James 2: 17*) In other words, not only did I believe I was now a new creation, but I put my belief and desire in to action. I said no to harmful substances, broke ties with anyone around me who was a negative influence, and began taking better care of my health. Most important, however, I put God back as number one in my life.

Today, I would like to encourage you to also make the change. Perhaps by honestly answering the following questions, it will help you see if today is YOUR time for positive ACTION.

* Are you happy with your life as it currently is? If not, what have you done to make things better?

* If you are in a relationship, is it one that is free from any form of sin and ungodliness? If no, what have you and the other person done to remove these impurities? If you both can't do it on your own, are the two of you willing to get help?

* Do you ask God to make things go your way, yet you ignore His call for repentance?

In the Bible, we are told that what you sow is what you will reap. (*"Be not deceived; God is not mocked: for whatsoever a man sows, that he also reap." -Galatians 6:7*)In more plain terms, we get out of life what WE put in to it.

The choice is yours.

Am I Really Saved?

I do not know you, and cannot see what is in your heart. However, God can, and His Word, the Bible, says that when you believe in Jesus Christ, and accept Him in to your life, you have eternal life.

"For if you confess with your mouth that Jesus is Lord and believe in your heart that God raised him from the dead, you will be saved." -Romans 10:9-10

The key word in the above verse is "believe." When we truly believe something we do not hide that belief secretly inside us, but we put that believing in to action. While some individuals express feeling a sense of peace and joy at the moment they accept Christ in to their life, others say they only began to feel differently when they truly began to apply their new-found belief in to their every day lives. States one man, "I realized that my temper and use of vulgar language would not be pleasing to God, so I began to apply God's sweetness and patience to those aspects of my character. You know what? People began to notice, and it encouraged me to be more Christ-like in other corners of my life! I can't even begin to tell you how much happier I now am!"

A middle-aged woman also replies, "I had committed adultery, and I was not being a very attentive mother. How could I continue in sin when I had just told God I wanted to start living better? It was difficult at first, but I ended my sinful ties and began to focus my attention on my marriage and children, now placing God at the head of my life where He should have been all along. With God's grace, and my sincere efforts, my whole family situation began to change! I love my husband and children, and I feel horrible for what I did, but thank God I am now washed clean of that sin, and a new creation in Christ! Only God could be so good!"

When we accept God and His Son, Jesus Christ in to our life, our reward is salvation and eternal life. However, there are other blessings and rewards; too many to list. The comfort and joy which stems from this divine relationship with our Creator is real and profound. The understanding that our sinful past is behind us, and we are now transformed, allows us to walk forward without shame or guilt. The name of God is now engraved upon our hearts, and the more we seek His truth, the greater this love and wisdom has the ability to bless our life.

Only you and God knows what is truly in your heart. However, if you are not saved, won't you invite Him in to your heart today?

Prayer: Heavenly Father, I desire to know You, and to find out what it is you require of me, and my life. I come before you kneeling because I am a sinner. I ask for You to wash me clean of my past transgressions so that I may become a new creation whose heart's desire is only to do what is good and right in Your sight. I thank you for giving me the strength and courage to let my actions speak louder than words so that I may never be ashamed of Your powerful presence within me. This I humbly ask in the name of Your Son, Jesus Christ. Amen.

Suggested reading: 2 Corinthians 5:17

Have You Backed Away From God?

"This righteousness from God comes through faith in Jesus Christ to all who believe. There is no difference, for all have sinned and fall short of the glory of God, and are justified freely by his grace through the redemption that came by Christ Jesus."
-Romans 3:22-24

The other day, I went to give my nineteen year old daughter a hug because I was happy to see her back home after a long day at work. However, when she walked in the door, and I cheerfully let her know her presence had been missed, rather than welcome my warm embrace, she backed off and let off a whiney, "Moooooom!"

The rejection stung.

Saying nothing, but feeling a tad hurt, I sat back down on the soft chair in the living room because I did not think it would do either of us any good for me to force myself upon her.

Immediately, God spoke to my heart and whispered, "Now you understand how I feel when people reject Me. I offer Myself freely to them, and desire to embrace them with My love, but all too often, I am rejected."

I quickly felt better, knowing that if God can handle the rejection of so many, then surely, I can cope with such temporary backing away from my own teen.

My dear friends, God is not a puppet-master who can manipulate us into having a relationship with Him. Every time we give in to what we know is wrong (sin), we are, in essence, telling God that His word and will for our life does not matter.

As the above Bible quote reveals, all individuals have sinned, and we all have fallen short of His glory. Thankfully, your heavenly Father is reaching out to you and calling you to a higher standard. Will you allow Him to embrace you, or will you back away?

Prayer: God, Thank you for helping me to see areas in my life where I may be turning away from You and Your divine truth and love. Soften my heart, Lord, so that Your word and will may be my desire.

This I ask in the name of Your son, Jesus Christ. Amen.

An Alzheimer's Story

"*L*ook at grandpa!" laughed Molly, "He put his pants on backwards! And I think they are wet too!"

"Shhh!" said mother quietly as she gently pulled her twelve year old daughter aside.

"Why does grandpa do funny things sometimes, mom?" asked Molly.

Mother let out a sigh, wiped her hands off on her apron, and knelt beside her youngest child. "Molly dear, I know you don't fully understand what Alzheimer's disease is, but it's something that older people occasionally get, and it sometimes causes them to be a little confused. That's why grandpa came to live with us; because he was sometimes forgetting to turn the stove off, and to take his medicine."

Just as Molly was about to respond, there came a big chuckle from the corner of the room. Molly's eldest brother, Freddie, who was a bit of a smart-aleck, had been hiding by the china cabinet and taking in the whole conversation.

"What mom's trying to tell you, Molly," quipped Freddie, "is that grandpa is nuts, so don't pay him no attention!"

Although mother was angry at Freddie's rude comment, more than anything, she was saddened. As tears rolled down her cheeks, she sternly said, "Freddie, that is my FATHER, and I will not have you talk to or about him in such a disrespectful or belittling way. Sometimes grandpa might not be fully aware of what he is doing or saying, but more often than not, he DOES know, and gets upset that he is having a hard time doing the things that used to come easy to him. Just because he has some dementia does not mean he no longer has feelings!"

Freddie's head now hung low. It was obvious he regretted his thoughtless remark.

Mother dabbed her eye with a tissue and continued, "Freddie, I want you to go to your room, and talk to God about this."

Without so much as a word, Freddie shuffled away, his little sister following.

Later in the afternoon, both Molly and Freddie walked down the stairs in to the kitchen where mother stood over the sink washing dishes. In his hand was a piece of paper.

"I prayed over the matter, mom, and I believe God showed me what I need to do," he said matter-of-factly.

"Oh?" said mother, "And what's that? Say sorry?"

"Well, that, yes, but more importantly, I believe God wants me to share this Alzheimer's prayer Molly and I wrote with other families too," Freddie continued as he fumbled with the piece of paper in his hand.

Mother turned around, wiped her hands on her apron, smiled, and replied, "Can I hear what you wrote?"

Freddie cleared his throat, straitened his posture, and read:

<u>An Alzheimer's Prayer</u>

Dear God, please help my family, friends and care-givers see me for who I always was, and not for what this disease has taken from me.

Help them to see that I want to be treated just like they do; with courtesy, respect and sensitivity.

Remind them, God, that although I may sometimes get confused, even act irrationally, these things can scare, frustrate and sadden me as much as it does them.

I don't want to be treated like a misbehaving

child. Let them know that the best thing they
can do during these times is to take my hand
lovingly and hold it or give me a warm hug,
for shows of love are universally understood.

Help my visitors to understand how grateful
and appreciative I am when they come and
spend time with me. I don't need presents, just
the precious gift of love. And just because I
may forget their name doesn't mean the love I
have for them in my heart has changed. I feel
it, and am comforted and warmed when I hear
their voice, see their smile, or feel their loving
embrace.

Let them know, God, that I don't like this
predicament any more than they do, and that
even though my needs are now different, I still
want to be included in their lives because, if I
lose my family and those dearest to me, then so
too will go my will to go on.
 I can deal with this disease because I have to,
but I just need them to be a little more patient
with me; a little more kind.

Lastly, help them, God, so we can get through
this together.

As he finished, Freddie looked up, only to find
mother sobbing; no longer tears of sadness,
but joy and pride!

"Oh Freddie! Molly! That is beautiful, and it is

a message that I hope everyone who has a loved one touched by dementia will hear!" exclaimed mother as tears flowed uncontrollably down her cheeks.

<u>Real Life Application</u>: Christ has told us to love one another, and treat each other as we would wish to be treated. As such, let us place His message into our hearts, and carry it out in to the world. His love will not only make a difference in how we view and relate to Alzheimer's patients, but also has the ability to transform lives, and soften even the most hardened hearts.

Invite love in.

Invite God in.

Change your life.

Change the world.

(copyright 2007 Melanie Schurr)

My Mother and I

*G*rowing up, my relationship with my mother was not as close as I would have liked. During those years I lived under my parent's roof, I didn't understand why our relationship was less than ideal, but once I became a mother myself, specifically a mother of teens, I began to see just how challenging motherhood can be.

While my own children are now adults, and have both flown the nest, I look back and wonder how I survived the 2 AM feedings, having little ones that were only 13 months apart, and recalling the time my husband and I were out to dinner, and our son decided to have a huge accident on my white pants, the odor forcing us to prematurely end our meal while customers around us requested different tables!

Or what about the time I walked in our children's bedroom, only to find our daughter's crayon scrawling all over the wall, and the day our son decided it would be neat to flush one of his toys down the toilet, necessitating a sudden call to the plumber?

Years passed, and before you know it, both kids hit the hormonal teens, and suddenly I was thrown back to the period my own mother and I seemed to have more friction in our relationship.

There is an old saying that goes something like, "You don't know what another person goes through until you have walked in their shoes." It was only when I was thrust in similar situation as my mother that I began to better understand.

Today, I am happy to report that my mother and I have a warm and close relationship. We still have our differences, but there is a certain respect and understanding of each other that, I guess, just needed time to develop.

In similar manner, our faith in God, and walk with Christ, also needs time to develop and mature. Just as we need to give ourselves and each-other a chance to grow and improve, so too must we do our part to nurture our faith because with God, all things are possible!

Do You Have "Blame-itis"?

 middle-aged man sat in a psychiatrists office. When asked why he was there, he told the doctor of this ongoing depression he couldn't seem to shake.

"When did you first notice this ailment?" asked the doctor as he rubbed his chin. The man replied, "I guess it began when my grown daughter began telling me what a bad father I had been."

"Have you been a bad father?" asked the psychiatrist.

The man sighed and replied, "I don't believe so, but she seems to think it."

The doctor scratched his head and then asked, "She didn't think this of you when she was a child?"

"No," replied the father as he wiped a tear from his eye. "We were always such a close and happy family. Our children were our life, and still are."

"Ah, I see," said the doctor as he jotted a few words in the pad of paper which sat upon his lap. "Tell me, and please be honest, were you or your wife physically, sexually or verbally abusive to her?"

"Absolutely not, Doctor. And that is why all of this is so frustrating and hurtful, because my wife and I held our roles as parents in the highest esteem, and made so many sacrifices for our children just so they could have a happy, safe and healthy life."

"What kind of things did you do together?" questioned the doctor as he again jotted in his notebook.

"Oh, we went on yearly family vacations, took our children to neat attractions, went sightseeing, etc." answered the father as his eyes began to light up.

"And what about on a daily basis; you know, the smaller things?" asked the doctor as he looked directly at the gray-haired man's face.

"It was those smaller things you refer to that were the joy of my life. I can't tell you how happy and proud it made me feel to walk in the door after a hard day, and smell a home-cooked dinner in the oven, and our children run to the door to greet me with hugs and shouts of 'daddy!'" he replied. "We'd go to parks, I'd play soccer with the kids, push them on the swings, we'd go on hikes, go to get ice-cream cones, my wife would help them

regularly with their schooling, science fair
projects, go with them sledding in the winter,
and to nearby parks after school. We gave our
best to our children because that is what was in
our hearts to do. Nothing was a chore because
just sharing in all these things brought my wife
and I so much joy."

"I'm listening," said the doctor assuredly.

The man continued, "Our daughter has had a
hard few years; getting into serious debt, her
husband left her for another woman, she got
two speeding tickets, and I suspect she may
now be turning to alcohol. Her mom and I
have tried to give her good advice, but she
doesn't want to hear it."

"Hmmm," said the psychiatrist, "I think I'm
beginning to see."

"See what?" asked the man.

"Well," replied the doctor, "It's a fairly
common malady I see a lot in my practice. It's
called "Blame-itis.""

"That sounds serious, doctor," said the man
with a puzzled look upon his face.

"Oh it is very serious because it zaps the
person who has it of their peace and joy, and it
can also be lethal to relationships!" the doctor

continued. "Blame-itis is what people get when they won't take personal responsibility of their own actions. Instead of accepting the consequences of what have been their own choices as an adult, they blame their problems on someone else."

The man offered a polite small smile, and replied, "I understand what you are saying, doctor, but how can I help my daughter?"

The psychiatrist took the man's hand and patted it, then stated," As a Christian, I believe the best thing we can do in such cases is pray; ask God to help your daughter see truth for what it is. Not everyone is ready for truth though, because truth can sometimes sting, but at the same time, it is also freeing. The next best thing you can do to help her is to just continue to love her unconditionally, letting her know that while you may not always agree with her choices, you still love her. Lastly, it is also important that you do not continue to allow your daughter's current state to affect you to the point of your own depression. Continue to be that loving father you were when your daughter was a child, and be strong for her while she is weak. If you both are weak, what good is that?"

The man stood up and smiled, saying, "I can't tell you how much your words meant to me, doctor."

<u>Real Life Application</u>: If any of the above purely fictional story rings true with you or someone you know, then let us focus on what Jesus Christ said of God's Word (the Bible), *"Your Word is the Truth ... If you continue in My word, you are truly My disciples. And you shall know the truth, and the truth shall set you free"* (John 17:17; 8:31-32).

Today, rather than be quick to blame someone, let us first look to ourselves and see if there is anything we may have contributed to the situation. Let us also consider being a bit more merciful, the way we ourselves desire God to be with us and our own shortcomings.

Our Furry Little Friends

I bet you may not be aware of the fact that in the US, the week of May 6th is "Be Kind To Animals Week."

The week often comes and goes unnoticed by many, but the message is still out that humans should treat animals well.

As an animal lover at heart, it amazes me that we need to promote such a message because it would seem common sense. However, we have all heard the news reports, or watched television programs which reveal pet owners who terribly neglect and abuse the very creatures they bring into their homes. What I probably will never understand is, why do people who have no genuine care for animals buy them? And, if they find they can no longer care for their pet, why can't they do the humane thing, and bring the animal to a shelter where it can be fed and placed up for adoption to a family who wants nothing more than to love this animal?

In my over eleven years of writing for Daily Wisdom *(DailyWisdom.com)*, the devotion which received the most reader responses was one in which I shared about my heartache over the loss of our beloved dog of 16 years, Otis. The love I had for him was real, and the grief I felt upon his death was also genuine. So many readers wrote to say they understood, for they have experienced similar emotions with their own pets as well.

Prayer: "Dear God, thank you for creating so many wonderful animals; the magnificent beasts who roam free in the wild, and the more vulnerable ones who look to us for kindness and care because they are now in our possession. Help us to be more sensitive to the needs of our little furry friends, and remind us to slow down the hectic pace we may be leading so we do not forget to give our pets the food, water and shelter from the hot sun, they need to survive. Soften our hearts, and open our eyes, God, so that when our pet is ailing or suffering, we will provide these animals with the same care we ourselves would hope for if we were sick and in pain. Lastly, I ask You, God, to come in to my heart and my life, to cleanse me of my sins, and help me start anew so that I may not only be a suitable pet owner, but more importantly, a better person who stands approved before You. This I ask in the name of Your Son, Jesus Christ. Amen."

Remembering Those Who Have Served

$\mathcal{W}$ithin the United States, "Memorial day" will be celebrated on May 28th of this year. The holiday commemorates U.S. men and women who have died while serving in the military for their country.

Many US citizens observe this holiday by visiting cemeteries and memorials, fly the flag outside of their own homes or place one at the grave of a loved one who served in the military, and have picnics or special gatherings.

As our 21 year old son and his cousin are still serving in Iraq at the time I write this devotion, Veterans day, Armed Forces day, Memorial day and Flag day, all which are US national holidays, will hold even greater meaning for our family.

It is good to fondly remember loved ones who have passed on before us, and especially good to pay homage to those men and women who have lost their life while protecting our homeland safety. However, what about honoring God, and recognizing and appreciating His sacrifice of His only begotten Son, Christ Jesus, and the many blessings He has bestowed on those who call upon His name?

You may not decide to do it today, but please don't put off a relationship with God, for He is truly worthy of our honor, respect and love.

Building Patience…and faith

$\mathcal{A}$lthough I didn't want to admit this to myself, I used to be a pretty impatient person. Mind you, I was not quick to temper, and was, in fact, quite a laid-back person, but when there was something I sought after, I wanted it IMMEDIATELY. Perhaps the best example is within my writing career. When I first seriously began writing apx. 20 yrs. ago, I wanted to be a good and well-received writer NOW. I didn't want to go through the years or rejections, fine-tuning and learning about the actual craft. I had things to say boiling within me, and my sole desire was to put pen to paper, and of course, in my dreams, my adoring readers would embrace these as gold.

Well, God had something else in mind because He saw the bigger picture which I and my lack of patience did not. I did have to go through years of rejections, receiving correction from those who traveled that way before me, and in the process, I began to develop better patience as well as skill. Meager newspaper 'letters to the editor' progressed to guest commentaries, which then grew to having my own column. One column blossomed in to another..and another, and then came magazine articles and appearances of my work on web sites. The next hurdle was a book, which would be an undertaking that would take years to complete because just when I thought I would be done, I'd want to correct this, or change the wording of a sentence here or there. Then of course, there was another 1-2 years it would take to send my finally completed manuscript out for it to hopefully be accepted by a publishing house. I would have to wait months or longer for their responses.

Several years ago, my first book hit the bookstores, and when I look back on this very long journey, I see that God used everything in my path to develop my lacking patience. Had He placed everything in my lap at once, I never would have been able to handle the responsibility. I am reminded of a fine wine that needs time to mellow and come to its peek taste.

How often in life are we all guilty of wanting what we want NOW…without thinking about if that is what is truly best for us, and without putting forth the effort to work toward that goal?

The same can be true with our relationship with God. We may say we want to know God, and be closer to Him, but we want it to occur immediately, and we blame God for ignoring or abandoning us if what we ask for doesn't happen as fast as we would like.

My dear friends, we may be able to get a hamburger and milkshake in a flash through the drive-through window of a fast-food restaurant, but we must never forget that faith is ACTION. Our Creator requires us to USE our faith as a seed which blossoms and sprouts roots that will hold firm in the ground. And, just as all seeds require water and time to grow, so too do we need the living water of God's word (the Bible) so that we can better understand God, His will, and what it is He requires of us. This is how our love for God deepens; because, the more we know Him, the better we love Him, and the better we love Him, the more our relationship with Him may grow.

Thankfully, we do not have to wait for God to come in to our life. All we need do is invite Him in to our hearts.

It may take time to read the Bible and to learn more about our faith, but we must take that first step by calling on God today.

Simply, Love

"𝒯eacher, which is the greatest
commandment in the law?" Jesus replied,
"Love the Lord your God with all your heart,
and with all your soul, and with all your mind.
This is the first and greatest commandment.
And the second is like unto it: 'Love your
neighbor as yourself.' All the law and the
prophets hang on these two commandments."
(Matthew 22:35-40)

What a simple act Christ asks of us, to love
God and each other, yet so many people find
this hard or even impossible to do. Their
reasons are many and varied. "I won't love
something or someone I can't see," says one
man. "My neighbor is an idiot! I can't love
someone like that!" says another individual.

If love is such a pure, natural and good thing,
then why is it so hard for so many of us to do?

In my view it is because man is a proud
creature. We want to believe we are self-
sufficient enough to be our own god so we
only have to answer to one being: ourselves.
Pride also disallows us from showing our
fellow man the grace to be imperfect, even
though we ourselves are not perfect. When a

neighbor, associate or family relation offends us, we may feel like hating, rather than loving this person enough to pray for him or her, even if that prayer is, "Dear God, please help to open her blind eyes!"

Loving each other does not mean we must act as doormats who take on another verbal or physical abuses. What is does mean is as the verse above suggests, treating others as you yourself wish to be treated. In other words, if we want others to offer us mercy and grace when we have done something stupid, we must likewise be willing to offer them that same kindness.

Regarding one's relationship with God, isn't it ironic that many people who have ignored God, when faced before immediate crisis, usually cry out to Him in despair? "Oh my God!" shouts one woman who just found out her son had been shot. Another person cries out, "Save me God!" when he is stuck in a terrible fire.

You see, my friends, when all is said and done, that is all there really is in this word; God and love. And, since God IS love, love is the perfect response.

Today, won't you bring love in to your life by inviting God in to your heart?

Open Arms

"The Lord is kind and merciful, slow to get angry, full of unfailing love. The Lord is good to everyone. He showers compassion on all his creation." - Psalm 145:8-9

Many people solely see our Creator as a fire and brim-stone God who is quick to anger, judge and condemn. While God does hold His children to a certain standard, as the above verse extols, He is a heavenly Father who understands man and his weaknesses even better than we know ourselves. As such, God knows our heart, and if our desire is to please Him and do good. Likewise, He also understands when we are hurting and in need of His grace, mercy and comfort during those times we must come to Him in repentance because we struggled or fell.

Just as your earthly father or mother would not just stand there and watch when you fell down and hurt yourself, our Heavenly father is even more loving and compassionate. He reaches His hand out to those who cry out to Him, and He is quick to forgive.

We all have made mistakes in life. Only God is perfect.

If you a person reading this who thinks that something you may have done is too much for God to forgive, <u>know</u> that He is ready and willing to welcome you in to His family with open arms.

Lost: One Missing Child

An article in our local newspaper told the gut-wrenching story of a family awake one morning to find their young daughter was missing. Days, then weeks passed, with no word or sign as to what became of their beloved child.

One can only imagine the pain and heart-break such families of missing children endure.

When we hear such stories, many of us say an immediate prayer that the lost child may be found healthy and safe. Sometimes this occurs, and when it does, we jump for joy because the lost child is back where he or she belongs.

Have you ever thought that this is what God must feel when one of His children is similarly lost?

Like any caring earthly parent, God is saddened when one of His little ones (you and me) have been lured away by the seducing ways of ungodly living. And, like that mom or dad who searches high and low for their missing one, so too does God never stop reaching out to us, and desiring our return back in to His loving embrace. Not so that He can condemn or punish us, mind you, but so that we can once again be back where we belong, safe and sound.

No matter what you may have done to cause
you to be 'lost,' God is ready, willing and able
to welcome you back in to His family. If,
rather, someone you know, is in need of
'rescuing,' won't you do your part and remind
them that their heavenly Dad is awaiting?

Self-Worth

*M*any people today question their self-worth, wondering such things as am I good-looking enough, do I weigh too much or two little, am I dressed fashionably, and, what do people think of me? The end result of such an ongoing personal attack are enhanced feelings of low self-esteem, decreased levels of peace and joy, and a general dissatisfaction with who we are as human beings.

Wanting to fit in may be common, but is it healthy to base what we do or say in life on this philosophy alone?

Absolutely not, and here is the reason why.

When we are preoccupied with ourselves focus is being taken off of where it should be directed: God. God desires us to live for Him, and to love one another, and treat each other as we ourselves wish to be treated. However, how can we do this if we are spending most of our time worrying about living up to societies often silly standards which tend to dictate that only the rich and beautiful succeed? Besides, whose version of success are we abiding by: man's or God's? If we are turning our back on people around us who may be hurting, and could benefit from our hand to hold or shoulder to lean on, because we are too consumed with our self, then perhaps it is time to readjust priorities.

When God is given the proper place in our life He deserves; right at the top, all other pieces of our life naturally seem to fall in to place.

Whose at the top of <u>your</u> list: God or yourself?

Mean What You Say

"Such persons claim they know God but from seeing the way they act, one knows they don't. They are rotten and disobedient, worthless so far as doing anything good is concerned." -Titus 1:16

several Atheists whom I have spoken with claim they want no part of the community of God because they don't like the hypocrisy they see; people who in word proclaim Christ's message of love, yet their actions sometimes tell a very different story. Of course I tell them that no man can compare to the one perfect God because we all have fallen short of salvation, and it is only by the grace of God that we are saved, but such words often ring hollow since one cannot truly justify hatred and disobedience.

I'm sure we all know someone who does exactly that; insists they believe in God, regardless of what sect they belong to, yet, they sometimes treat others cruelly, and judging them unfairly and harshly based on skin color, nationality or something else which identifies them as being 'different.' We may know that God desires us to love one another and treat others we ourselves wish to be treated, but if this is the case, they why do we sometimes utter hate-filled remarks as, "Oh, you know how those people are; not well-bred and very uneducated!" Or, "I don't mind them, but I wouldn't want one of my kids to marry one!"

Then of course, there is the type of hatred and disobedience some of us even display when we are driving our cars on a busy highway, being quick to anger, lacking patience and kindness, and muttering curse words and using vulgar hand gestures that insult God and the faith we claim to hold dear.

This list could go on and on, but I am sure you get the point, that being, not only is someone always watching, even when we think they are not, but how we behave can either be a positive testament of our faith, or a way in which to turn people off from wanting anything to do with such nastiness and hypocrisy. This is something we all are guilty of at one time or another, myself included.

If you have been living the life of a Christian in name only, won't you recommit to the faith by making today a better day, not just for yourself and God, but for those around you whether they be friends, loved ones, associates or complete strangers?

If you have not yet made the decision to invite God and His son, Jesus Christ, in to your life, won't you give those of us who may have disappointed you another chance in much the same way God is willing and able to forgive you and let you begin anew?

He is indeed a God of positive transformation!

Reach Higher!

"…live no longer as the unsaved do, for they are blinded and confused. Their closed hearts are full of darkness; they are far away from the life of God because they have shut their minds against Him, and they cannot understand His ways. They don't care anymore about right or wrong and have given themselves over to impure ways."
-Ephesians 4:17-19

*M*any people hear the term "born again" yet don't really understand what it means, perceiving it to reflect someone who is an extremist or fanatical.

The term "born again" merely represents a rebirth; from abandoning ones former sinful ways, and embracing a straight and narrow path where Christ may be glorified. It is a rebirth of mind, body and spirit.

What glorifies Christ?

Goodness & righteousness: living Christ's message of love one another and treat others as you yourself wish to be treated.

As the above Bible verse reflects, if we have released sin's hold on us, it only makes sense we will no longer live as those who continue to walk in darkness, rejecting God and His credo of love. Such people cannot comprehend this message because their hearts are hardened, and their desire is not truly toward knowing what is right and wrong. Instead, their life philosophy is one dominated by the selfish and lustful desires of their own will, and flesh, not spirit, is given priority.

God calls us to reach beyond our flesh and blood and to trust His mercy, wisdom and abilities.

If you are already a Christian, yet you are not fully convicted to your faith to the point of where your actions speak just as loud as your words, today is a good day to recommit your life to Christ.

If you would live to experience this rebirth; abandoning sin, and grasping on to God's good ways, follow the links at the end of this page so you may receive additional resources. Feel free to contact me as well, at editor@MelanieSchurr.com

I love to hear when someone has decided to reach higher!

A Brand New Day

"…Christ has given each of us special abilities--
whatever He wants us to have out of His rich
storehouse of gifts." -Ephesians 4:7

$\mathcal{A}$s the silver-haired woman walked up the
long drive she could see him peering through
the window. Every day it was the same thing,
she would come to clean up the house, and he
would just sit there in his wheelchair staring
out the window. Oh, he could speak alright,
but I suppose he simply chose not to. And,
who could blame him? Ever since the accident
5 years ago, the once familiar faces that used to
fill this large home with such life, began to
slowly drift away, much like his once positive
attitude.

"Good morning, sir," Helen, the house-keeper
stated as she walked through the door.
Charles, the 35 year old paraplegic whose
domicile it was, grunted. "Cat got your tongue
again today, sir?" retorted Helen coyly as she
began to put away the dishes on the counter
which the night nurse could never seem to
manage on her own. Again, Charles simply
grunted and continued to stare out the
window.

The day progressed and Helen went about dusting, polishing, sweeping and washing. It was a particularly dreary afternoon due to what seemed like was an all-day rain. Feeling her mood drop a little, and knowing how much a good ditty raised her spirits, Helen turned on the radio, going from station to station trying to find just the right song. Just as she found a robust polka, suddenly a loud roar pierced the melodic tones coming from the radio. "Turn that garbage off!" demanded Charles, his face contorted with anger. Helen was so caught off-guard by the sudden strong display of emotion that in her attempt to quickly turn the radio off, she accidentally broken the no completely off. With polka music now blaring, Helen momentarily stood expressionless, then, all of a sudden her lip began to crinkle, then tremble, and then, from the depths of belly came the most delightful and prolonged laugh! Glancing over, Helen could not believe her eyes! Her wheel-chair bound boss was also chuckling!

Upon composing themselves, and unplugging the radio, Charles used his eyes to motion Helen to come near him. Helen knelt near his wheel-chair to ensure they could face eye to eye. "I am so very sorry for yelling at you, Helen," stated Charles as stared intensely at the elderly woman's face. " I don't know what came over me, not just at that moment, but ever since I've been a prisoner to this wheelchair. Hearing the music was yet another cruel and painful reminder of what I have lost, and never will have again." Helen didn't say a word, but merely held Charles limp hand and listened. "At one time I used to love music, dancing, reading, and the arts in general. All of that died when I became paralyzed. Look at my life now. I have nothing." Tears began to roll from Charles' eyes.

Helen let go of Charles hand, and began to dig through her purse, immediately grasping a tiny framed picture. "Look at this picture, and tell me what you see," she quietly asked Charles as he looked at her puzzled. "It's blank. Nothing is there. It's just white," replied Charles. Helen smiled subtly, and said, "Oh no, sir. It is a beautiful snow fall, or perhaps it is a fluffy white cotton ball, or a crisp white bed sheet hanging outside on a line outside to dry." She continued, "That picture is like one's life. Either it can remain a blank canvas, or we can make something beautiful and meaningful out of it. The choice is ours." "No," said Charles, "I didn't have a choice. My choice was stolen away!" Helen smiled again and quietly said, "I beg to differ, sir. You still have choices, but you just need to be a bit more creative by digging a little deeper so you can see what those choices may be."

Charles now clung to her every word. "I don't

understand what you mean. Please explain."
Helen thought a moment then her eyes lit up.
"You like music and dancing, right, sir?' "No,
I USED to enjoy dancing to good music!"
abruptly stated Charles. "No, sir, if you loved
it once, you will still love it, but remember
what I said, be creative!" stated Helen
assuredly and she moved his one "good"
finger over the switch that made his electric
wheel-chair move. She then walked over to
the radio and plugged it back in to the wall, the
robust polka music still playing. Up and down
went the click of Charles's switch, and back
and forth went his wheel chair. Charles smiled
richly, then clicked the tiny lever to the right,
then left, and round and round went his wheel
chair! "Look Helen! I'm dancing! I'm dancing
to the music!" Helen nodded, grinning from
ear to ear, as she reached over to momentarily
stop Charles chair from moving two and fro.
"There's more, sir," stated Helen. "Remember
how, before your accident you always used to
say how you loved being around little children
because they were so full of promise? Well,
there is no reason why you can't still live out
that dream by being a little creative. You may
not be able to push a child on a swing at the
play ground, but the local library has been
searching high and low for someone to fill the
part-time position of story-teller in the
children's reading room."

For the first time in a very long time, within

Charles eyes, Helen could see life and hope.
She did all she could to keep her own self from
crying at that moment, however, these would
be tears of joy.

With new, bright eyes, Charles asked, "Helen,
how did you get to be so wise?" Helen looked
down to her arm, and slowly began pulling up
her sleeve, soon to reveal tiny numbers
permanently marked on her skin. "You see,
sir, when I was a little girl, my entire family
died in a concentration camp. I was the only
survivor, and I had no one, not even an aunt or
uncle. Like you, I felt like I too had everything
important taken away from me, and my future
seemed very bleak. A kind couple adopted me
shortly after that, and while I of course still
missed and loved my family, I came to also
love them for they showed me that we all are
special in God's eyes, and we also have special
gifts that we need to discover and use so that
we too can help others. It is this circle of giving
and receiving that life is all about." Helen then
reached in to her purse again to fumble with
the tiny framed picture. "They are the one's
who gave me the tiny white picture many
years ago, and before I left for college they told
me that what that picture reflects is up to ME."

Charles sat motionless, once again staring
momentarily out the window, then stated with
newfound resolution, "Helen, tomorrow is
going to be a brand new day! The beginning of

my new life!"

<u>Spiritual application</u>: As the above Biblical verse reveals, "Christ has given each of us special abilities" and it is up to us to use these gifts for the good of mankind. For some people, that gift might be the ability to be a teacher, good public speaker, author, doctor or nurse. For others, it might be someone who has special way of dealing with and helping people, be it, a day-care provider, baby-sitter, or retired grandparent who volunteers time at the local community center helping young children to swim. Regardless of what our life circumstance is, God's desire is not for us to abandon these gifts merely because times may get tough, but instead, as the above story reflects, for us to be creative and find ways to continue on giving in way form or another so that we can not only be more fulfilled living, but more importantly, so that He and his word may be glorified.

Tomorrow CAN be the beginning of a brand new day.

Intentions

 $\mathcal{T}$ here is a saying which goes, "The path to Hell is paved with good intentions." How true this is for when we sin, it is not usually our intent to hurt and disobey God, but isn't that exactly what happens?

Think about the young man sitting in prison for shooting another man. "I never intended to shoot the gun! I just wanted to scare him a little but I guess my anger got the best of me," the man states as he stares at the cold dank walls of his jail cell.

Or what about this one? "I didn't intend to be unfaithful, but it just sort of happened!" replied the middle-aged woman to her marriage counselor.

Or this? "I walked into the store intending to simply shop, but once I saw the diamond ring and how beautifully it sparkled…well, I figured no one would notice if I slipped it in to my pocket," stated the young woman as she tried to explain her crime of shoplifting to the police officer.

The problem with sin is that rarely does it initially expose itself for what it truly is: evil. Instead, purposeful deceit is reduced to nothing more than a "little white lie," while the sin of adultery masks itself as a night of so-called harmless fleshly pleasures, and viewing pornography is justified as harmless titillation.

My dear friends, we need to beware of sin, and learn to quickly recognize it for what it is. It doesn't matter what our intentions are, because the true proof to our walk with God is if we will flee from sin, or if we will walk toward it.

Today, if you are someone whose intentions have been misdirected by the lure of sin which presents itself as sweet, but in reality is putrid and decaying to your soul, please know that God is merciful and forgiving to those who repent and seek His good way.

"Dear God, I know I have made mistakes, some of them very serious. I also know that you came, not for the perfect, but for the imperfect. I have made some bad decisions, but now I am ready to make those right by walking away from the evil that has so bound me. I am ready to make You, not sin or my own flesh and selfish desires, Lord of my life. I ask you to forgive me, God, and wash me clean of my sins. I ask You to make me a new creation that is pleasing in your sight, and to show me how to have more strength and wisdom so that I can better recognize evil where it lurks. This I ask in the name of your son, Jesus Christ. Amen."

Pro-life

"This day I call heaven and earth as witnesses against you that I have set before you life and death, blessings and curses. Now choose life, so that you and your children may live." -Deuteronomy 30:19

The term pro-life may sound familiar to you since those people who oppose abortion commonly utilize this term to reveal what they believe is a sanctity of life. This does not mean that those holding a pro-life view do not also place great importance towards the life of the mother. For Christians, it is not a matter of choosing to support either the mother or child, but rather, a respect for the life of both as we all are God's precious children, and an innocent baby should not have to be put to death simply because we made a mistake.

The term, pro-life, also defines our walk with God; whether we will choose good over evil, and salvation over damnation. Turning our back on God, and succumbing to the ways of satan do not promote life, but in fact, destroy and corrupt.

The world is filled with both good and bad. Choose life and be blessed!

Are you someone who has not always

respected life, and are seeking forgiveness from a past poor decision you now deeply regret? Remember, Christ came for the imperfect, not the perfect, and as such, there certainly IS mercy and grace to those who call upon the Lord in repentance.

Let today be the start of new day, and a new way.

More! More! More!

"Their destiny is destruction, their god is their stomach, and their glory is in their shame. Their mind is on earthly things." - Philemon 3:19

No pun intended, but obesity is a growing problem. Whether it is adults or children who over-eat way beyond the point of satiating hunger, and then combine this with a lifestyle which has little physical activity, this mind-set of "More! More! More!" is causing great un-health amongst the world's masses.

Some people are gluttonous with food, and others want "More! More! More!" of other things that can be just as harmful, such as abuse of alcohol, and seeking an over-abundance of material items.

I don't know why we have this notion that if one is good, 100 will be better! In other words, a glass or two of wine with dinner is lovely and good for digestion, but one person drinking the whole bottle in a single sitting is over-doing it. Same thing is true with material goods. It's perfectly fine to want nice things, but do we really 'need' to own 20 pairs of sun-glasses, 150 pairs of shoes, and enough jewelry to start our own boutique?

Some people even over-do it where their jobs are concerned, and they are so focused on getting "More! More! More!" from their career, that they may not even notice that while they are climbing the ladder of success, their marriage is falling apart, and children are running amuck.

Our heavenly Father, God, wants us to enjoy life and be healthy, but one needs wisdom to be able to discern between what is healthy desire, and what is greed and gluttony.

Today is a good day to break those chains of bondage which may be weighing you down. Let God be your strength, hope and light at the end of the tunnel.

Priorities

"If you are risen with Christ, seek those things which are above, where Christ sits on the right hand of God. Set your affection on things above, not on things on the earth." -Colossians 3:1-2

How ow easy it is to get caught up in the stresses of daily living. After all, there are rooms to be cleaned, meals to be cooked, jobs to be attended to, money to earn, children to drive to school, relationships to deal with, and, this list could go on and on. During this time when we may be planning, even worrying about such things, many of us completely forget that God has a place in our lives. Those who do remember God, may only place Him on the backburner; not giving Him the best of our being, but basically just giving Him the few left-over measly morsels of our hectic schedules.

Since we live on this earth, and are of course, earthly beings, it is a fact we do need to take care of our, and our families earthly needs. However, as the above Bible verse reveals, our primary "affection" (heart and love) should be on God above.

"That's ridiculous!" you may say, "Am I supposed to ignore my other areas of life on earth just so I can honor God?"

No. God loves you and your family, and wants your utmost health and happiness. It is not a matter of choosing one over the other, but placing one's priorities in order. When we place God at the head of our life, like pieces of a puzzle, everything else seems to naturally fall in to place. This is why God wants our focus to first be upward.

In my own life, I try to look heaven-ward as much as possible because I know that God wants this type of intimacy with me. Just as an earthly father wants a close relationship with his child, so too does God want us to know that we can come to Him for things both large and small.

When something or someone is number one in our life don't we allow this to be our driving force?

Yes, and if God is given the place in our life He deserves, it is also only natural that we will seek to nurture that love by feeding it well, and doing what we can to make it flourish!

God's is ready, willing and able to pour out His love upon you in a very big way! Won't you invite Him in to your heart and home, and make Him #1 in your life?

Be Happy With What You have

"You shall not covet your neighbor's wife. You shall not set your desire on your neighbor's house or land, his manservant or maidservant, his ox or donkey, or anything that belongs to your neighbor."
-Deuteronomy 5:21

As the above Bible verse conveys, we should be content with what we have and not covet those things our neighbor has that we do not.

Why do you think this is?

Of course God wants us to reach higher and make the best life for ourselves, but what 'we' may regard as 'the best' is not always what God holds as important. For example, we may love our spouse, but yet we might compare them to our attractive neighbor, or the lady at the grocery store, and the man on the cover of the sport magazine. "If only my wife lost 30 lbs., then we'd have a better relationship," you may say. Or you might think, "Hmm. How much happier my life would be if I had more money!" Or you may say in conversation, "Oh! What I wouldn't give to drive one of those fancy European sports cars!"

Once again the question begs to be asked why

some people, rather than count the blessings they already have, instead focus on what they don't have, or what could be bigger and better.

It is nice to want the best things in life, but let us not forget that what God considers important and good are not always the things which hold priority with mankind. Gold, diamonds, furs, fancy cars, big homes and spouses with the bodies of Adonis and Venus hold no relevance to God, or our walk with God. Certainly God wishes us to be in good health and to prosper, but it is the nourishing and riches of our spirit that matters most to God.

Today, won't you consider placing material and shallow things to the wayside, and ask God to instead bestow upon your heart the desire to instead richly feed your spirit?

Bible Versions

A young girl states, "I tried reading the Bible but I just don't understand it!"

This teen is not alone. In fact, the first time I read the Bible, I had a hard time as well.

As a much younger person, a friend suggested that each time I pick up the Bible, first pray. He told me, "Ask God for wisdom, knowledge and understanding so that His word may become a living reality in your life." My own suggestion is to use a version of the Bible you are comfortable with.

All Christian Bibles extol the same message, but depending on what version you use, the wording may be a little different, although the basic sentiment remains unchanged. For example, an Old English version may state, "I thirst." Yet, another version may declare, "I am thirsty!" Still another version may state, "I need something to drink!"

Some people believe there is only one version of the Bible to use, but in my opinion, if a particular version better assists you in coming to and knowing the Lord, then go for it! Besides, our faith is not from a book, but exists within the living word of God which is impressed upon our heart.

Won't you open <u>your</u> heart and mind to your creator today?

Through Example

$\mathcal{W}$e worry so much about how pretty our form is, if we are wearing the right make-up and fashionable clothes. We also are concerned about how tight our abs are, and how good we look from behind.

Wanting to be fit and healthy is well and fine, but many of us make the mistake of being more concerned how others see our physical entities than give careful consideration to what type of example our words and actions may reveal to those around us.

A model may have stunningly good looks but when dealing with people she may be self-centered and thoughtless.

The man in the three-piece business suit who seems externally well-polished may also be cheating on his wife, and neglecting his children. So too, many the seemingly sweet mother-in-law have a sharp and vulgar tongue behind closed doors.

Yes, people are watching, but not just at how our external facades appear. They also witness the true contents of our character, and just because someone has not brought your attention to a character flaw does not mean such weaknesses do not exist. Even when you think no one is around, God is ever-present and all-knowing, and there is no fooling the King of kings, and Lord of lords.

Today, won't you ponder making the change from unrighteousness to righteousness? God is watching…and waiting for you.

True Love

" *Teacher, which is the greatest commandment in the law?*" *Jesus replied, "Love the Lord your God with all your heart, and with all your soul, and with all your mind. This is the first and greatest commandment. And the second is like unto it: 'Love your neighbor as yourself.' All the law and the prophets hang on these two commandments."* -Matthew 22:35-40

*M*onths ago, I wrote a Daily Wisdom on the above simple act Christ asks of us; to love God and each other. Following, a reader wrote to say that I made reaching out in love sound too easy, and that there are times doing so is not humanly possible, or will be done with teeth gritted.

Below is my response to him.

"Contrary to your own opinion, I do believe 'love' is the response Christ calls from us. Love is also one of our most basic emotions, and yet, as you point out, far too many people believe it must be distributed reluctantly and with 'teeth gritted,' almost as if we are being forced to do something we really do NOT want to do.

That is not love, for love comes from the heart, and it is able to see through the hurt, pride and ego, because it understands the bigger picture. That bigger picture or end result is that where there is love, all things are possible.

To your point though, true, no one said it would always be easy, but as I mentioned above, this is most often because we are letting other things (ego, pride, hurt) get in the way.

Another point to mention is that loving one another does NOT mean being someone's doormat. Love also speaks the truth (in love), and thus can be sharper than even a double-edged sword. This is why Christ calls us to wisdom and understanding; so we can know how to apply love in all its various forms.

Here is an example.

Years ago, when our teenaged son was in the hilt of raging puberty hormones and challenging our parental authority on a regular basis, my husband and I gave him a choice: adhere to our house rules (minimal respect and civility) or you will be asked to leave.

Of course we wanted him to stay, but setting boundaries and daring to discipline was our way of loving our son. If we did NOT love him, we would let him run around wild. So you see, not ALL forms of love are warm and fuzzy. Some applications can have a definite sting.

It is the same thing with truth spoken (in love). Hearing the truth can often sting, but as the Bible says, it will set you free! ("Then you will know the truth, and the truth will set you free." -John 8:32)

Another example.

A woman is drinking heavily every day. Someone who truly loves this woman will speak the truth to her, and tell her she is an alcoholic, and needs to get help before the booze kills her. These are not the sweetest words she may want to hear, and she may even get very angry, but months later, when she is recovering and feeling more clear-headed, there is a good chance she will realize this was an act done in love.

Back to your point. If we are loving begrudgingly, then is that really love?

In my opinion, no."

Today's Daily Wisdom is on the beauty and healing power of love. When love (in all it's diverse forms) is practiced, all things are indeed possible!

Never Satisfied

"I am not saying this because I am in need, for I have learned to be content whatever the circumstances." -Philippians 4:11

𝒮arah was an intelligent and loving middle-aged mother of three adult children. Richard, her husband of twenty-nine years, was a devoted husband and father who worked hard to climb the corporate ladder so he could provide for his precious family.
Sarah was never interested in working outside the home. Her raising of three little ones always kept her busy, and then there was her baking skills which allowed her to run her own little home business, catering to small parties and gatherings. The money they jointly earned was not enough for them to be regarded as wealthy, but they were comfortable within their average income bracket.

Or so they always thought.

For the last few years, Sarah had been thinking a lot about how nice it would be to have all their bills paid off. Her motive, which began innocently, was simply to take some of the financial burden off her husband's shoulders. However, what began as a loving thought slowly began growing in to thoughts of how great it would be to own a yacht, fully-loaded RV, have an in-ground pool, and the rest of their yard professionally landscaped. Sarah would also page through magazines, and dream about how much nicer the house would look if they bought better quality furniture, and did this or that renovation.

"All I need is more money," whispered Sarah quietly to herself.

Sarah scratched her head and began thinking about how she could obtain more money without putting any further pressure on Richard.

"I've got it!" she said as she stared at their dog, Barney. "I'll start playing the lottery!" Before long, Sarah's simple buying of one lottery ticket went to her spending $30.00 a week, for in her mind, she was sure this would greatly increase her chances of winning the big one. When that didn't happen, Sarah began going to the casino on the other side of town. Sure, she won some small pots, but with the hope of winning something even larger, the small winnings were simply put back into her habit, and each time Sarah would leave the casino with an empty wallet.

More and more, Sarah was finding herself depressed, which she tried hard to hide from Richard and the children. Not only did she feel like her dreams might never come true, but now she was also frustrated over all the money she had needlessly lost.

One day, just as tears began to flow, Richard's car pulled into the drive, and Sarah quickly rushed about to dry her tears and compose herself. Shortly after, as the family sat around at the dinner table, Richard replied, "Honey, I'd like to make a special blessing." Sarah and the three children bowed their heads and listened. "Dear God," began Richard, "I was just thinking today about how good you have been to us! I have been getting so caught up in my job that I think I forgot to slow down and not only stop and smell the roses, but see the roses as well! I am so rich, God, and I have been too blind to see and appreciate how wealthy I truly am! We may not have fancy furnishings, or live in a mansion, and we may never be able to afford diamonds and furs, but of what I truly need, I have it all! I thank you, God, for the roof over our heads, the clothes on our backs, and the food on our table. But most of all, I thank you for the most precious gifts in my life, my wonderful wife and children, and Your divine presence! I thank you for this in the name of Your Son, Jesus Christ. Amen."
With that, Sarah began to sob uncontrollably. It was like a burden had been lifted from her shoulders, and a veil removed from her eyes. How foolish she now felt for not being content with all that she had.

<u>Real Life Application:</u> Our Heavenly Father understands our desire to better our life. There is no wrong in having goals and dreams. However, there is a difference between need and greed.

A philosophy of "More! More! More!" is an unhealthy one because it is satan, not God, who wants to rob us of our joy, peace and contentment. (*"Be self-controlled and alert. Your enemy the devil prowls around like a roaring lion looking for someone to devour."* -I Peter 5:8) (*"The thief comes only to steal and kill and destroy; I have come that they may have life, and have it to the full."* -John 10:10)
If we are always wanting more, then we will never be satisfied.

Today, I urge you to ask God for something. Not furs or gems, fancy cars or designer outfits, but rather, for something far more precious: a relationship with Him.

Tug Of War

"If any of you lacks wisdom, he should ask God, who gives generously to all without finding fault, and it will be given to him." -James 1:5

$\mathcal{W}$hen I was a small child I used to love playing tug of war. In case you are not familiar with this simple game, one or more individuals pull on a long piece of rope which has a tie in the middle of it, and each side's goal is to try to pull the other side past a line that has been marked on the ground. The side with the longer end of rope wins.

Did you know that we all are involved in a game of tug of war? Not a fun game, mind you, but a spiritual war between the forces of good and evil.

"Put on the full armor of God so that you can take your stand against the devil's schemes. For our struggle is not against flesh and blood, but against the rulers, against the authorities, against the powers of this dark world and against the spiritual forces of evil in the heavenly realms." -Ephesians 6:11-12

As the above Bible verse suggests, we need to be cautious and take heed so we do not unwittingly fall prey to Satan's wiles. Part of the spiritual armor we must prepare ourselves with is wisdom.

Why wisdom?

Because we need to know who the players are; who is the good guy, and who is the bad guy. Since satan is a deceiver, he will use tactics which may make us think his ways are the right ways, but they are not, for as the Bible reveals, his purpose is to steal away our salvation.

"Be self-controlled and alert. Your enemy the devil prowls around like a roaring lion looking for someone to devour." -I Peter 5:8

Wisdom is so important that the Bible refers to it as better than precious rubies!

"For wisdom is more precious than rubies, and nothing you desire can compare with her."
-Proverbs 8:11

Prayer for Today: "Dear God, please help me to see the importance of spiritual wisdom so that I may walk down Your straight path always. Wash my soul clean of all ungodliness, so that I will instead hunger and thirst for ways that are pleasing to You. Help me to turn my back on sin, and stand strong against temptation, but most of all, let the truth of Your word give me wisdom so that I may live that glorious life you

have in store for me! This I ask in the name of
Your Son, Jesus Christ. Amen."

For Those Who Suffer

"My comfort in my suffering is this: Your promise preserves my life." -Psalm 119:50

𝓗ave you ever wondered why bad things sometimes happen to good people?
In the Bible, the Scriptures state, *"Now if we are children, then we are heirs of God and coheirs with Christ, if indeed we share in his sufferings in order that we may also share in his glory. I consider that our present sufferings are not worth comparing with the glory that will be revealed in us."* (Romans 8:18)

Sometimes, people have a tendency, when reflecting upon the life of Christ, to focus solely on Jesus' gentle and loving nature-- how he called children to his side, and performed wondrous miracles. What about how the Son of God suffered when he was rejected by man, mocked, betrayed and denied by his friends, was falsely imprisoned, spat upon, beaten, and finally, crucified?

"He was despised and rejected by men, a man of sorrows, and familiar with suffering. Like one from whom men hide their faces he was despised, and we esteemed him not." (Isaiah 53:3)

The fact is, if, as the King of King and Lord of

Lords, the Son of God endured suffering during his time on earth, then we must not wonder why we, God's children, may likewise face hardships and unfairness within our lifetime. However, as the above verse suggests, the bumps along the path we face on earth are nothing compared to the glory that will later be revealed to us.

During times of adversity within my own life, such as times I may feel let down by a friend or loved one, or times an unfairness may come my way, I stand and look at a plaque I have which is a piece of wood with two long railroad spikes prominently displayed. The rusty and thick old spikes remind me of the nails which pierced Christ's flesh. I recall the pain, humiliation, sadness and other very real human feelings he endured at the hands of man, and it is not long before my own 'suffering' or 'persecution' pales by comparison.

There are times when unfortunate or unfair circumstances simply befall us. However, sometimes we create our own pains and hardships, and the suffering we endure is the result of our own life choices; our rejection of that which is good and right.

Today, ask God to help you see your life truthfully so that you may understand the nature of any hard times you may be going

through. Invite God in to your heart, and ask Him to wash you clean of any transgressions, even in the form of ungodly mindsets.
There is a glory that awaits the children of God, and it is up to you to partake of it!

Have I Told You?
(A poem)

*H*ave I told you that I love you, and how
special you are to me?

Do you know exactly what I feel for you,
and that when I'm in your presence I feel joyful
and free?

Have I told you of all the wisdom you have
passed on to me over time?

Ah, the things I took for granted, but now they
are no longer mine.

I miss the little things about you, and I'd give
anything to again see..

...the smile of your face, and your arms
wrapped around me.

But, you are now gone, and it is too late;
was it an accident, or was it fate?

Death came quick, and now here I stand;
reaching out and hoping you will take my
hand.

I wish I could turn back the hands of time, but
that simply cannot be,

so I am left to wonder,

"Have I told you that I love you, and how special you are to me? "

Real Life Application: There is an old saying that goes, "Absence makes the heart grow fonder." The reason this is, is because it seems a common occurrence to better appreciate the good we had when it is no longer around. In short, we tend to take for granted life's many blessings; including the gift of love.

As we enter into a new year, let us resolve to make truth and love reign supreme. May we leave no loving word thought of, unspoken, and let there be no unfinished business; for the time to speak and show the truth of our love to friends and family is now!

Today is the day to set aside petty differences, and long-held bitterness; to release things of the past we cannot change, and to embrace the present and future by starting anew!

Likewise, we must not delay reaching out to or making amends with our heavenly Father, God, for He alone, is the original source of truth and love.

Our Comforter

*H*ave you ever sometimes felt alone, overwhelmed by whatever situation is troubling you, and that no one truly understands the pain you feel?

Someone DOES understand: God.

"He was despised and rejected by men, a man of sorrows, and familiar with suffering. Like one from whom men hide their faces he was despised, and we esteemed him not." (Isaiah 53:3)

As the above Scripture reveals, the Son of God was a man of sorrows; one who was familiar with suffering. While Jesus was loved by many, there were also those individuals who despised Him, and did not see or appreciate Him for the special Being He is.

How wonderful it would be when we are feeling low to have someone who loves us, come to us and embrace us with such satisfying love and comfort that we can KNOW that no matter what comes our way, they will be there to see us through it. How sweet the words, "Do not worry. I am there with you, and we will get through this together," would be!

My dear friend, the comfort we all seek now and then is already here! It has been right there before us, yet not all of us partake!

His name is Christ Jesus, and He is a comfort to all who call upon Him in sincere repentance.

"Have I not commanded you? Be strong and courageous. Do not be terrified; do not be discouraged, for the LORD your God will be with you wherever you go." -Joshua 1:9

Street Preacher Mike

"For the Lord gives wisdom, and from his mouth come knowledge and understanding."
-Proverbs 2:6

𝒯wo elderly women were window-shopping and strolling downtown. A small commotion in front of the local soup kitchen caught their attention.

"What's going on?" asked Helen.

"Oh, that's just street preacher Mike talking to the young people!" replied Bertha, a stout, white-haired lady. She continued, "He's been coming here for at least ten years, and everyone just seems to love him!"

Helen watched in amazement because she had never seen so many young people seem so interested to hear the word of God.

"Let's go watch," said Helen as she grabbed Bertha's arm and urged her closer to the gathering.

Being a former school teacher, Helen was impressed at how wise beyond his years street preacher Mike was. The words he spoke touched the core of her heart, and she just knew this had to be a man who spent much of his life in college or seminary, gaining theology degrees, and the like.

When street preacher Mike finished, Helen quickly approached him. Grabbing his hand and cupping it with the other, she stated, "What a wonderful job you do here! What university did you attend? I bet your parents must be very proud of you!"

Street preacher Mike smiled gently, and replied, "Well, thank you ma'am, but I've never known my parents. The closest thing I had to parents was a nice teacher I used to have in elementary school who took a special interest in me. And, I regret to say that while I would have loved to attend college, I didn't have the means to do so. "

Helen patted street preacher Mike's hand, and said warmly, " There is the knowledge one can obtain within the walls of a school, and then there is a type of wisdom that comes from one source alone; God. You may not have known your earthly father, but your heavenly Father certainly knows who you are!"

Street preacher Mike nodded, and before he could say another word, a young girl yelled out, "C'mon preacher Mike! We're waiting for you!"

With that, the two new friends smiled and parted ways. However, as Helen and Bertha crossed the street, Helen suddenly remembered something the street preacher said, and immediately yelled out, "Pastor! What was the name of the elementary teacher you said was nice to you?"

Street preacher Mike waved and then shouted, "Helen! Her name was Helen!"

Real Life Application: How wonderful that God does not require us to first gain a degree before we can begin to reap the awesome benefits of His divine wisdom, and allow His truth, love and light to transform our lives!

"My son, if you accept my words and store up my commands within you, turning your ear to wisdom and applying your heart to understanding, and if you call out for insight and cry aloud for understanding, and if you look for it as for silver and search for it as for hidden treasure, then you will understand the fear of the Lord and find the knowledge of God." -Proverbs 2: 1-5

I Love Spring!

*E*ver since I was a little girl I have loved Spring. Of course, living in the north-east portion of the United States at the time allowed me to experience the diversity of the seasons in all their glory!

At the house I grew up in was several lilac trees which, at the onset of Spring, gave off the most delightful perfume which scented our entire front yard. Likewise, new sprouts of brilliant green grass would also fill the air with such a clean and fresh aroma!

In our back yard was a pond and creek. How exciting it was to see frogs, grasshoppers and butterflies return to their mossy home after the cold of winter, and to hear the trickle of the creek water splash over the rocks!

I recall thinking how everything seemed so clean, fresh and new in Spring: a time of new life!

Did you know that God, through His great love and mercy, can provide His children a rebirth and renewal of His own?

"But when the kindness and love of God our Savior appeared, he saved us, not because of righteous

things we had done, but because of his mercy. He saved us through the washing of rebirth and renewal by the Holy Spirit, whom he poured out on us generously through Jesus Christ our Savior..."
-Titus 3:4-6

That's right, my dear friend! When we accept Jesus Christ, the Son of God, as our Lord and Savior, and denounce the past effect of sin in our life, God so completely spiritually cleanses us that our slate is literally washed pure and clean: we are new creations!

"...let us draw near to God with a sincere heart in full assurance of faith, having our hearts sprinkled to cleanse us from a guilty conscience and having our bodies washed with pure water. Let us hold unswervingly to the hope we profess, for he who promised is faithful." -Hebrew 10:22-23

Prayer: "Dear God, I know I've done some bad things in my life that have hurt You, myself and others. I am ready to set the past aside, and to begin anew. I believe You sent your Son to die for me on the cross for my sins, and that through His resurrection I may have eternal life. Wash me clean of my sins, God, and create in me a new heart. This I ask in the name of Your Son, Jesus Christ. Amen."

Know Your Foundation

*E*aster is a time for Christians to come face to face with their faith. Our foundation, which rests in Christ Jesus, is presented through the son of God's death and resurrection. For this reason, Easter is not just a holiday, but more importantly, a holy day.

Just as we may become so caught up in the festivities of dying eggs, Easter egg hunts, purchasing chocolates for baskets, and planning the traditional ham dinner, that we may miss or not give this holy day its just benevolence, it is equally common for Christians to miss some of the messages taught within its own cherished Scriptures.
The most misquoted Bible verse is, "Money is the root of all evil."

Money is evil, you say? How can that be when money can buy food to feed the hungry, pay for the medical care of the sick and dying, and when donated to noble arenas can help fund necessary scientific research for the betterment of mankind?

If this makes no sense to you, it is because what the Bible really says is, *"For the love of money is the root of all evil."* (Timothy, 6:10)

Now that makes sense! After all, think about why most crimes are committed. Someone is trying to beat the system for the sake of personal gain. The robber, mugger, and wife who is hiring the hit man to knock off her husband who has a large insurance policy, all are willing to do the unthinkable so that they may somehow easily cash in. Morality and common decency is set to the wayside, and it is their love of money that allows the almighty dollar to become their god. This is the evil, not money, per say.

Scriptural misquotes can even be used to support racism, making it appear the Bible supports not mixing the races. The argument goes something like this, "Even God says we should not be unequally yoked!" Sorry to disappoint any KKK supporters out there who use this distortion to condone their own hatred and ignorance, but this particular verse in 2 Corinthians 6:14 refers to believers marrying unbelievers. Such a hook-up is regarded as being "unequally yoked" because, logically speaking, there is an unevenness or division of beliefs.

"Be ye not unequally yoked together with unbelievers: for what fellowship hath righteousness with unrighteousness? And what communion hath light with darkness?"

Think about it. If dad is an atheist, and mom is

a Roman Catholic, by whose belief system are they going to raise little Johnny? "Oh, we will just raise him to be open-minded and be exposed to the best of both worlds, then he can make up his own mind," is the common reply. Sounds easy, but when put in to real life application more often than not fails miserably because Johnny is getting mixed messages from people whose duty it is to care for and guide him. Then, when little Johnny gets older, whose belief system is going to dominate when its time to decide if Johnny attends a public school, or enrolls in a private Christian institution? Will Christmas and Easter be celebrated for its true spiritual significance, or will secularism win out, and Christ born and risen tossed to the wayside?

Obviously, such an "unequally yoked" marriage would have great obstacles to overcome, that is, if they could be overcome. In this case, either husband or wife would have to compromise their own faith in order for resolution to be found, and the probable growing resentment could be disastrous.

My dear friends, if we believe that the word of God is the will of God, then perhaps it would behoove us to take more time to see what our Creator truly has to say, rather than to pass on worn misquotes that have a semblance of truth, yet are not fully accurate. Just as one cannot understand a novel by letting it simply gather dust, or merely reading a few pages here or there, likewise, the Bible must be opened and read before its significance can be withheld.

Admit It!

$\mathcal{E}$ver since my mid-forties I have noticed some subtle yet significant changes about me. My energy level isn't what it used to be, I tire more easily, my pace seems to have slowed a bit, (ok, a lot!), and keeping fit and trim has become a real challenge.

Challenge?

That's putting it mildly!

Ok, I must come clean. I need to lose a good thirty pounds!

If you think that is easy for me to publicly reveal, you are wrong, and I know that the majority of women especially reading this Daily Wisdom, will be able to relate to what a sensitive and often embarrassing issue this can be for us females.

Admitting the truth about ourselves isn't always easy because it forces us to come face to face with our flaws, inadequacies, and perhaps even our sins.

No one wants to admit they are a liar, thief, adulterer, greedy, given to lustfulness and sloth, but without this type of reality check we will remain lost in behaviors and mind-sets that are destructive to our self, others, and most of all, our relationship with God.

Prayer: "Dear God, I am ready to look in to the mirror. Please show me the truth of who I am, even if it stings. Give me a new heart, God. One that hungers and thirsts after righteousness, and whose desire is to please You. I am ready to shed the former, and to reveal the cleansed and renewed. This I ask in the name of Your Son, Jesus Christ. Amen."

No Flashlight

"For these commands are a lamp, this teaching is a light, and the corrections of discipline are the way to life.." -Proverbs 6:23

$\mathcal{A}$ young man went out from his back yard at night in hope of finding worms for the following day's fishing trip. He had lived in this area for many years, and seemed to know every nook and cranny, so saw no need to take a flashlight with him. "The light of the moon was good enough for my grand-pappy, so its good enough for me!" he thought to himself as he treaded down the long and narrow cobblestone path which lead from his yard and in to the grassy field behind his home.
Sure enough, an hour went by and the young man indeed found his fill of night crawlers, knowing just were this and that rock or stump was located to look under. He'd lift the rock, and as soon as he saw that familiar wriggle, he'd quickly snatch the worm for its next mornings duties.

Just as the young man decided it was time to return, he spied a large log. "Just one more," he thought.

As usual, he pushed the moss-covered log over with his boot, and upon seeing that familiar wriggle, plunged his hand down... only to let out a shrill scream! What he grasped was not a night crawler, but a small snake! He had been bit!

As he could not see what type of snake it was, the young man dropped his jar of worms, and ran like a mad-man out of the field, tripping and falling along the way.

Real Life Application: Chances are, if this young man had brought a flashlight with him he would have been able to see the danger ahead.

Most of us don't intend bad things to happen, but they can, and do, especially when we are unprepared and approach certain matters unwisely. We may think we have everything under complete control, and fully understand the consequences to our words and actions, but do we?

As the above Bible verse implies, God gave us His word to provide us with wisdom; to act as a light in a world of darkness. Just as it is unwise, even dangerous, to walk at night without a suitable light source, so too, should we invite and allow God's illumination to guide and protect us throughout our life.

Paint Jobs

I was recently thinking about my now-deceased grandmother, and how genuinely sweet she used to be. For a few moments, I closed my eyes and tried to imagine her cozy home which was so neat, clean, and always seemed to smell of some sort of wonderful dish she was baking. Suddenly, my mind then drifted to a very small act grandma did which most people probably over-looked, yet I, even as a child, found subtle amusement.

Grandma had this old fashioned wooden bench in the hallway of her home for as long as I could remember. She and all her many guests and family relations would briefly sit upon it while taking off their boots which had become damp or soiled from the intense Buffalo (NY) weather. I suspect grandma must have picked that item up used from a yard sale, as it was obvious the bench had many coats of paint on it. Yet, several times a year, grandma would repaint it, due to its easily chipping and peeling paint.

Anyone who knows anything about painting is aware that in order for paint to best adhere to a surface, it is necessary to remove built up layers of old paint. I recall an uncle or two offering this information to grandma, but on she went painting that silly bench several times a year.

I am reminded of how many of us often do the same thing. We may adorn ourselves in such a way that gives others the impression we are pretty and new, offering polite smiles and kind words when we know someone is closely watching, yet, not far from the surface exists facets to our character that are quite ugly. We may claim to be new creations, yet under that fancy exterior is a heart which may harbor hatred, resentment, lack of forgiveness, thoughtlessness and other characteristics to our persona God would find displeasing.

Just as my grandmother needed to remove the old paint, and not simply cover up the old with the new, so too must we release the ugly grip of sin within our lives. It is not enough to just talk the talk. We must walk the walk, not just at times we think someone important is watching, but rather, what we claim to believe and hold dear must be at our very core.

Prayer: "Heavenly Father, cleanse me of my transgressions, and make in me a new heart; one that thirsts after those things which are good and pleasing in Your sight. Help me to teach others about You and Your goodness, by my own example; how I live my life, because, before I can take Your light out in to the world, I must first truly place it within me. "

Think Positive!

"The thief comes only to steal and kill and destroy; I have come that they may have life, and have it to the full." -John 10:10

There have been some disturbing things in my life lately. Nothing serious or life-threatening, mind you, but more like little annoyances, to which, when combined, have the ability to affect one's mood.

Maybe you can relate to how bits of negative gossip that find their way to your ear can be hurtful? Or, how one can feel frustrated over a strained relationship? Maybe your own situation is different, and what is affecting you is worry, stress or fear?

After a few weeks of feeling not at my best, it finally sunk in to my brain that, in life, there will always exist joy-zappers, (whether they be people or events), but it is up to us to decide if we are going to allow such situations or individuals to so intensely affect our life that we are no longer as happy and at peace as we can be.

As the above Bible verse reveals, Jesus Christ came that we may not only have life, but have it to the full! However, it is not the Son of God who attempts to steal away and rob us of the abundant and glorious life He desires for His children.

If we chose to dwell on negativity, every aspect of our life will reflect this. But, if we lay all that is bothering us in God's capable hands, and tell Him the desires of our heart, our heavenly Father

"...is able to do exceeding abundantly above all that we ask or think according to the power that works in us." (Ephesians 3:20)

It's Up To You!

A really great Bible verse that is often overlooked is, *"If you can believe, all things are possible to him that believes."* (Mark 9:23)

The reason I like this verse is because I think many people who don't believe in God tend to say such things as, "There is no God. If there was, He would not allow this to happen!" when life does not go their way. I find this ironic because they seem to blame a Being they don't even believe in for not granting the desires of their heart.

Why is it that God is often held accountable for our own lack of belief and faith?

The key word in the above Bible verse is YOU. Meaning, it is up to YOU to believe, and if YOU can believe, then all things are possible to YOU who believe!

It appears to me that some people simply go about their daily lives waiting for God to just dramatically jump in or make that first miraculous move. The sun rises and falls day in and day out, and still they wait for something to change, but it never does.

When will we realize that God's hand is always

outstretched to us, but it is we who have refused to take hold?

Make tomorrow a better day; let it be the first day of your new life in Christ.

It is up to YOU.

The Melody Of His Love

$\mathcal{U}$pon going through my CD collection in an attempt to find that just right type of music, one that would reflect my then current mood, it occurred to me that after many years of buying a disk here and there, my collection had grown quite vast. While some people have one or two types of music they prefer, mine represents styles from numerous diverse cultures and genres. When I am feeling particularly energetic, I play classic rock, disco, or something from a foreign land which has a lively beat one could dance to. During times I feel like singing, I reach for a Broadway musical, and when pensive, I put on something intense, such as classical, or something with a Latin flavor.

It certainly does seem like music has the ability to provide something for everybody. An individual may not care for opera, but they may adore alternative music. Or, someone may be deeply moved by folk music, yet another person may not be able to appreciate its earthy roots.

In similar manner, there are those people who have made an attempt to read the truths presented within the Bible, but because they may have been unmoved by the particular chapter or verse their eyes gazed upon, they decided God's word simply wasn't for them.

My dear friends, if you wouldn't totally abandon listening to and enjoying music just because you didn't care for a certain style, then why do we often so easily do this to God; turn our back on our spiritual welfare simply because we may need a little help understanding and appreciating the Scriptures? Or what about those people who make an effort to attend their local church, yet find the experience was less than what they expected, and thus, decide to never step foot in a church again?

Friends, the fact the Bible was not written by one person, and was the work of numerous divinely-inspired men and women of God, shows that God appreciates diversity. In His eyes YOU are a unique creation!

If you are someone who has given up on God due to what you perceive as a bad or lacking experience, please join me in the following prayer:

"Dear God, Please help me to know You, and be closer to You in a way that I can appreciate. Help me to not base You on what may have been the flaws of man. Lastly God, give me patience so that I will not be so quick to give up on You again. "

Christmas Around The World

*B*y time this daily devotion is published, my son, who is in the Armed Forces, will be celebrating Christmas in Iraq. Knowing this, I began to wonder about how other peoples of the world celebrate the birth of Jesus.

I was surprised to find out that in Christian homes in Iraq, on Christmas eve, one of the children in the family reads the story of the Nativity from an Arabic Bible while the other members of the family hold lit candles. Once completed, a bonfire made of dried thorns is lit in the home's courtyard, and a psalm is sung around it. On Christmas day, a similar bonfire is built in the church, and the bishop holds a replica of the baby Jesus, then continues on with a long service and blessing of the congregation, known as "the touch of peace." In the traditional Russian Christmas, there is prayer and fasting, sometimes for 39 days, (until January 6th, when the first evening star in appears in the sky). A 12 course feast, in honor of each of Christ's apostles is had. On Christmas Day, songs are sung, people gather in festively decorated churches, and another special dinner is enjoyed.

Christmas in Mexico begins with "La Posada," a procession which reenacts the search for shelter by Joseph and Mary before the birth of Jesus. The red star-shaped poinsettia flower is displayed, and the story passed down through the generations that a boy walking to church long ago to see the nativity figures had no gift to place before the Christ child, so he gathered plain green branches which miraculously bloomed as he set them down by the nativity scene. On Christmas day, children gather their gifts of candy from a pinata. Children deemed as "good," also receive a gift on January 6th, in memory of the "three wise men." Most Mexicans attend a midnight mass (la misa del gallo) and sing lullabies to the baby Jesus. Regardless of your cultural background, may all the peoples of the world sing Christ's praises on the day they set aside to acknowledge His birth! Let the feasts be had, and the rooms gaily decorated, for God gave to us a Savior who is King of Kings and Lord of Lords!

In closing, let us read about Christ's birth as revealed in the book of Luke (chapter 2) of the Bible:

In those days Caesar Augustus issued a decree that a census should be taken of the entire Roman world. (This was the first census that took place while Quirinius was governor of Syria.) And everyone went to his own town to register.
So Joseph also went up from the town of Nazareth in Galilee to Judea, to Bethlehem the town of David,

because he belonged to the house and line of David. He went there to register with Mary, who was pledged to be married to him and was expecting a child. While they were there, the time came for the baby to be born, and she gave birth to her firstborn, a son. She wrapped him in cloths and placed him in a manger, because there was no room for them in the inn.

And there were shepherds living out in the fields nearby, keeping watch over their flocks at night. An angel of the Lord appeared to them, and the glory of the Lord shone around them, and they were terrified. But the angel said to them, "Do not be afraid. I bring you good news of great joy that will be for all the people. Today in the town of David a Savior has been born to you; he is Christ [a] the Lord. This will be a sign to you: You will find a baby wrapped in cloths and lying in a manger." Suddenly a great company of the heavenly host appeared with the angel, praising God and saying,

"Glory to God in the highest, and on earth peace to men on whom his favor rests."
When the angels had left them and gone into heaven, the shepherds said to one another, "Let's go to Bethlehem and see this thing that has happened, which the Lord has told us about."
So they hurried off and found Mary and Joseph, and the baby, who was lying in the manger. 17When they had seen him, they spread the word concerning what had been told them about this child, 18and all who heard it were amazed at what the shepherds

said to them. But Mary treasured up all these things and pondered them in her heart. The shepherds returned, glorifying and praising God for all the things they had heard and seen, which were just as they had been told."

Your Priority List

"But seek first his kingdom and his righteousness, and all these things will be given to you as well."
-Matthew 6:33

$\mathcal{N}$ow that the new year is upon us, many people with the best of intentions have begun to put their new year's resolutions in to practice. Bob, the mailman, has vowed to quit smoking, and Sandra, the beautician, has pledged to devote more time to her children. Likewise, Dr. Marshall, is determined to learn a new language, and Martha, his receptionist, is making losing fifty pounds her priority in the new year.

It's wonderful to desire better for our lives, and the start of another year certainly gives one a good excuse to start anew, however, with all the promises, hopes, resolutions and intentions, somewhere along the line many people have forgotten to consider the most important decision of all; the start of a new relationship with God.

When God is situated at the head of our life as He deserves, everything else naturally falls in to place. The Bible confirms this: *"Blessings crown the head of the righteous, but violence overwhelms the mouth of the wicked."*

(Proverbs 10:6)

Scriptures also confirm that if your earthly parent knows how to give gifts to one's (earthly) children, then don't you think your Heavenly Father, God, can bless HIS children even exceedingly more abundant above all that we ask or think?

Of course!

"If you then, though you are evil, know how to give good gifts to your children, how much more will your Father in heaven give the Holy Spirit to those who ask him!" (Luke 11:13)

Prayer: Dear God, I don't know where to begin, but I do know that I need to start somewhere, so why not today, here and now? I have sinned, God, and I have turned my back on You. I am truly sorry for everything offensive I have done against You, myself and others, and I am ready to change my ways. I ask You, God, to wash me clean of my transgressions, and give to me a new heart; one that thirsts for righteousness. From this moment on, it will be the start of my new life in Christ!

Stand!

*I*n her regular opinion piece, a local columnist asks the question, "When is it time to stop the handouts?" The writer is referring to young adults, and the doting parents who continue to "help" them long after they are children, by paying off their college expenses, gas cards, cell phones, car-insurance payments, rent, and, well, you get the picture.

To the individuals being "assisted," I am sure the "helping hand" brings a smile and sigh of relief, but the truth of the matter is that spoon-feeding individuals who are capable of feeding themselves robs them of far greater gifts. Being an adult is about more than being legally able to drive, or by proving an age requirement on one's identification card. It is similar to how a mother bird gently pushes her baby from the nest so that her little one can learn to fly and gather food alone so that he may survive when she is gone.

So too do our own grown children need to experience such responsibilities as paying off their own bills and being personally and financially accountable for their own actions or they will remain forever reliant on mom and dad, (or grandma and grandpa), and that is far from what being an adult is about. There are psychologists who go so far as to say that such pampering behaviors are a form of control. Both my husband and I moved from our parent's homes at a young age. Both of us worked hard, and for the most part, supported ourselves. When I couldn't afford something, I did without it. I suppose I could have ran and asked my parent's, but I wanted to prove to them, and more importantly, myself, that I was responsible enough to handle my own affairs. The sweet result was that the self-sufficiency made me appreciate everything I worked for all the more. I didn't wear brand name clothes, or eat filet mignon, but the self-respect and confidence which came as a result was worth more than gold!

This Daily Wisdom is not about advising parents to not be there for their grown children when they really need it because there are times in life we ALL need a helping hand and shoulder to cry on. However, just as there is a time when we must encourage our children to stand on their own, so too does God require each of us to come to Him willingly and lovingly, not out of coercion or guilt, but of our genuine desire to have a one-on-one relationship with our Creator.

Stand, and walk forward. God is waiting for you.

Always In My Heart

"*T*hat's a pretty necklace, Grandma. Where did you get it?" asked young Melody as she fiddled nervously with her pigtails, adorned with bright yellow ribbons. Grammy Rose felt the pendant which clung around her neck, and replied, "Oh, that's from Grandpa Jake. He gave it to me many years ago as a small token of his love and affection."

"Do you love Grandpa a lot?" asked Melody curiously.

Grammy Rose smiled and immediately replied, "Oh yes, dear child! We have been married for nearly forty years, and if something ever happened to him, I just don't know what I'd do!" She cleared her throat and quickly added, "Enough of that now, child. Let's tend to our chores!"

Years passed, and the day Grammy Rose hoped would never arrive came. Melody, now nineteen years old, escorted her beloved grandmother to the coffin of her dearly departed husband. Grammy Rose seemed to be in a deep emotional haze, almost as if she was in shock. Melody squeezed her grandmother's wrinkled hand and whispered, "He is gone in earthly form, Grammy, but his love for you is

still close to your heart."
Melody was not quite sure why she said this,
but the words just came to her, and she hoped
they would be comforting.

Months passed and Grammy Rose still
remained in a deep and dark abyss of grief and
loss. Seeing her extreme weight loss, frail
appearance, and terribly neglected home,
Melody prayed that God would show her how
to help her broken-hearted grandmother. As
she and Grammy Rose sat at the kitchen table
sipping a cup of chamomile tea, the sun grew
suddenly bright. Grammy Rose squinted. Just
then, Melody noticed how the sunlight made
the necklace Grandpa Jake gave Grammy so
long ago sparkle. A huge and knowing smile
came over Melody's face. "Grammy, years ago
you told me Grandpa Jake gave you that
necklace as a small token of his love for you."
Grammy Rose nodded as she grasped the gold
heart pendant tightly.

Melody continued, "I noticed the chain hangs a
little low; almost over your heart."

Grammy Rose's eyes widened as she carefully
noted the chains location. "I was so happy to
receive it that I guess I just never paid attention
to that part."

"You know how Grandpa always paid such
close attention to detail, Grammy. It wouldn't

surprise me if when he bought this for you, it was his intent for the heart to not only be a reminder of his never-ending love for you, but for you to never forget this love will live in your heart always. In other words, his love is close to you even now!"

Still holding the pendant tightly over her chest, Grandma Rose's countenance changed. It was as if a crushing weight had been lifted off her, and hope was renewed. Through tears of joy, Grammy Rose replied, "Oh Melody! You are so right! How could I have forgotten this? My love for your grandpa IS still in my heart, and there it will stay forever! You are right! His body is gone, and I will surely miss him, but I know his spirit is with the Lord, and one day I will see my beloved husband again! In the meantime, the love is still within my heart, and I will do my best to allow it to comfort and sustain me!"

Melody quickly stood, and went to the other side of the table to where Grammy Rose sat. Leaning down, she gave her sweet grandmother a firm embrace. From that moment on, Melody knew Grammy Rose was going to be OK.

<u>Spiritual Application</u>: During times of great duress it is sometimes easy to feel so overwhelmed that the thought of a brighter tomorrow seems nowhere in sight. It is at these

times, we may forget that God and His great love for us is still present and available, and it is this love which may allow us to overcome pain, suffering and adversity.

The main character in the above story understood that the heart pendant from her husband held no special power, but that it was intended to be a reminder. In her case, the small token of her husband's affection was enough to remind her of the power of true love.

This Daily Wisdom is intended to be a reminder to you, the reader. Have you neglected your faith? Maybe today is a good day to place God in your heart.

Tell Me About Heaven

"*M*om," asked Sam, "Do you really think we will see dad again?"

"Yes, Sam. I do," she quietly replied as she placed her hand on her teenaged son's shoulder.

Sam was an only child, and his father meant everything to him. From the time he was small, his father was an active and positive influence on his life. As such, when his father became ill, it was startling to see him so weak and fragile. Watching him die was the worst, for it made Sam feel helpless. Through her tears, Sam's mom whispered, "Death is an unfortunate part of life, Sam. God will give us strength to deal with this."

Later that night, Mother went to check on Sam. As she sat on the edge of the bed, she began to stroke his hair. "You know, Sam, your dad loved you very much, and since the Bible says that love goes on forever, we can find comfort in that knowledge."

"And now these three remain: faith, hope and love. But the greatest of these is love."
                                        -1 Corinthians 13:13

Sam wiped a tear from his eye and turned to face his mother. "Tell me more about heaven, Mother."

"Well, " Mother began as she cleared her throat, "Heaven is where God is. The joy there is beyond anything we can even comprehend or imagine."

"Eye has not seen, nor ear heard, nor have entered into the heart of man the things which God has prepared for those who love Him." -I Corinthians 2:9

Mother continued, "In heaven there is no death, sadness, sickness, or poverty."

"And God will wipe away every tear from their eyes; there shall be no more death, nor sorrow, nor crying; and there shall be nor more pain, for the former things have passed away." -Revelation 21:4

Sam's eyes widened as he asked, "So, Dad will be happy and in no more pain? That is very good then!" Sam continued, "What will Dad look like in heaven?"

Mother smiled and then quoted a verse from the Bible which she remembered comforted her greatly when her own father died, *"The body that is sown is perishable, it is raised imperishable; it is sown in dishonor, it is raised in glory; it is sown in weakness, it is raised in power; it is sown a natural body, it is raised a spiritual body. If there is a natural body, there is also a spiritual body. " -1* Corinthians 15:35-44.

"It is good that we be in our spiritual forms in heaven, Sam, because our physical bodies as we know them are flawed. As you are aware, flesh can become aged and diseased, and sin also affects us. I do know that we will know one another in heaven because Jesus referred to it as paradise, and what kind of paradise would it be if we couldn't even recognize our loved ones?"

"Jesus answered him, "I tell you the truth, today you will be with me in paradise." -Luke 23:43

"And don't forget that after Christ's death on the cross, then resurrection, although there was a little confusion with some of his friends and loved ones, most of them immediately recognized him."

"You know, Mom," said Sam as he placed his hand on top of hers, "It is a comfort to me to talk to you about these things. I think my sadness is more because I will miss seeing and talking with Dad, but I think I will be OK since my faith lets me know he is in a much better place: with God."

Mother leaned over and tightly embraced Sam, "Your father would be so proud of you!"

"Thanks, Mom," whispered Sam. "And your Father, God, would be proud of you for reminding me about my faith!"

Real life application: Our time here on earth is so short. That time also tends to go very fast as we involve ourselves in our families, career, social life and hobbies. The reality is that we do not know when sickness, disease, or unexpected accident may occur.

Do not put off a relationship with God and His son, Jesus Christ, until time of tragedy. Today is the day to create new hope and be assured through faith of your heavenly reward.

"Not everyone who says to Me, Lord, Lord, will enter the kingdom of heaven; but he who does the will of My Father who is in heaven." -Matthew 7:21

Show Your Love

ℰver since my brother died unexpectedly last summer, I am more keenly aware of how, in the blink of an eye, a loved one can suddenly leave us. In hindsight, I wish I could turn back the hands of time and do and say so much more with him, but death is not so accommodating. While in some situations we have the opportunity to prepare for someone's parting, such as an elderly relative who is in critical condition in the hospital, more often than not, death comes when we least expect it. The end result is often grief tinged with regret. "If only she could have known how much I loved her," sobs one mother whose teenaged daughter died of a drug overdose. "I feel bad because I kept putting off spending time with him," says a young man whose father suddenly passed away of a heart attack.

The time to show those you care about that you love them is when they are alive, not when they are dead and gone.

Many of us are far too guilty of allowing petty frictions get in the way of what is truly important, and before you know it, time has passed, calls are missed, and visits are canceled.

My dear friends, not only is today a wonderful day to let our loved ones know they are appreciated, but it is also a perfect time to create a stronger bond with your heavenly Father. Just as you can set aside those small differences of opinion that may strain your earthly relationships, so too can we make the decision to release sin from our lives, and cleave to those things which are good and pleasing to God.

Do you love God?

Then show Him!

God and Gossip

A few of my relatives seem to have a very hard time keeping a confidence. Mention some sort of difficulty you are having, and before you know it, it has become the new topic of local gossip. While such individuals may make wonderful reporters at the local TV station or newspaper, divulging private matters to the public can oftentimes be very hurtful, as most of the time such stories end up traveling right back to the ears of the person they concern. To make matters worse, additional embellishments can also make a proverbial mountain out of a molehill.

While those near and dear to us can sometimes greatly disappoint us by not treating our private communications privately, what is said in prayer by us to our Creator, God, is always treated as the gift it is. I assume this is because, unlike man, God is not a flawed being. He has no hidden agendas, speaks only truth, and fully understands the contents of our heart. I suppose this is one of the reasons I enjoy prayer so, since I know that what is said between God and I, goes no further.

My dear friends, are you hurting or carrying some sort of secret inside you? Then tell it to God, and unload your burden on Him!

Our Own Happiness

*Q*ur nineteen-year-old-daughter is coming to better understand that, for the most part, we are the keepers of our own happiness. For years Lindsey has been bothered by her excess weight, and while she expressed a desire to be in healthier physical shape, she did little to change what obviously displeased her. When she would come to me expressing frustration at her inability to lose, I would say, "You CAN be healthier if you want to, but you have to be in the right mind frame. When you really WANT to do it, you WILL."

I am proud to say that this truth has finally hit home with Lindsey, and she is slowly but surely reaching for a higher health standard for her life. She has already lost twenty-two pounds!

Lindsey relayed to me how difficult it was at first to reach for a salad instead of a greasy pizza, or to say, "No thanks," to the sweets and treats she had enjoyed in the past. However, it is obvious to see that once she gathered up the motivation and turned her desire in to action, the payoff was not only improved health, but a sense of accomplishment which, of course, boosted her self-confidence.

Just as it took our daughter a while to understand the cause and effect of bad eating habits, so too do many people wrestle with issues in their own lives which rob them of the peace and happiness they could be having. Sadly, it is often by their own hands and wrongful choices.

The time to break free and reach for that higher standard is today! Yes, God is good, and He is indeed miraculous, but it is OUR responsibility to choose sickness over health, and goodness over sin.

Is something bothering you, pulling you down, and robbing you of the ecstatic life you could be living? Then look upward, my friend. Call out to God, and ask Him to give you the strength and motivation to change what is inward.

Positive change is a decision away.

Tell It To God!

An elderly man grumbles, "I left the Church because all they wanted to focus on were feel-good topics like peace and joy! I wanted to hear more of the old fire-and-brimstone type sermons that my grand-pappy used to preach! These youngsters of today have no fear of Hell, and that is what they really need!"

A young woman complains, "I really got away from my faith because it was such a turn-off to hear about the dangers of sin and Hell. I wanted to hear more about Christ's teachings on love and forgiveness. Topics like that make me feel good!"

There is an old saying that goes something like this: "You can't please all of the people all of the time, but you CAN please SOME of the people SOME of the time."

I suspect this is why the Scriptures were not divinely-inspired by one sole individual; but rather, numerous men and women of God who each had unique ways of relaying the same truth. While one writer may prefer a more direct and confrontational approach, another may communicate a similar message in song, psalm or more flowery language.

Perhaps God knew that diverse ways of communicating Scripture can be as unique as its reading or listening audience, regardless of whether one is hearing Biblical truths within the four walls of a church, taught within the home by parent to child, or read over the Internet in a medium such as Daily Wisdom. To focus on only one aspect of the Scriptures does the whole work injustice. One cannot preach of Christ's joy, without also speaking on His tears and suffering. So, too, can we not talk only about life, without also considering the realities of death.

The truth of the many diverse Bible subjects may not always be what we want to hear at any given moment, but I believe that if a topic is important to God, then it should be important to us.

Do The Right Thing!

*S*ometimes I wonder if the fear of being "politically-correct" or not intruding on an individual's "diversity" may be preventing the truth of God's word, the Bible, from being revealed to the masses.

Perhaps we don't want to step on anyone's toes or risk offending someone by sharing with them information God clearly says they need to hear. (*"Therefore go and make disciples of all nations, baptizing them in the name of the Father and of the Son and of the Holy Spirit"* -Matthew 28:19)

My dear friend, if we do not want God to be ashamed to call us His children, then likewise, we should not be ashamed of Him and His word. It is not for us to judge His message as presented in the Scriptures, but to simply do as He has asked, for we are not here to please man, but God. (*"On the contrary, we speak as men approved by God to be entrusted with the gospel. We are not trying to please men but God, who tests our hearts."* -1 Thessalonians 2:4)

I am reminded of a period in time when many people said nothing about racism and prejudice due to fear of speaking out, and standing up for what was right. The result of this inactivity was that evil was allowed to continue on.

When you care about someone, you warn them if they are about to stumble off a cliff. And, if you see an individual about to drink poison which he thinks is lemonade, you likewise make certain they know that sipping the beverage will lead to their sickness and demise.

If this is the case, then why, dear friend, are we often fearful and hesitant to share the truth of God's word with a world that so desperately needs to hear it?

Some people will accept God's word, and others will reject it. Doing so may cause us to make friends, or enemies. However, truth is truth, and it is God's business, not our own, for as the Scriptures affirm, "*For we do not preach ourselves, but Jesus Christ as Lord, and ourselves as your servants for Jesus' sake.*" -2 Corinthians 4:5

Taking a stand for the truth, and doing what is right is not always easy. In fact, in this day and age, it can be quite difficult at times because what God has to say on a given subject may not always match with our current society's view. For example, man may say that having a sexual relationship outside of marriage is not a big deal, but God's word declares adultery as sin. ("*Marriage should be honored by all, and the marriage bed kept pure, for God will judge the adulterer and all the sexually immoral."* -Hebrews 13:4) Likewise, our friends may tell us its acceptable to lie, cheat and steal, but is this really what God would have us do? No, it is not always easy to do the right thing, but the rewards which come as a result are more than well worth it!

The Ultimate Gift Of Life

"*I* am sorry, Mr. and Mrs. Blackstone. We tried our best, but the damage was too severe," whispered Dr. Korbet to the distraught parents who received a call in the middle of the night informing them their son had been in a car accident. He continued, "This is a terrible time, but if you wish to donate any of your son's organs, I will need to know as soon as possible."

Deciding upon organ donation was the last thing the Blackstones wanted to think about. Their only child, Matthew, was only seventeen years old, and a life that was so full of promise had now been tragically ended at the hands of a drunk driver.

As the parents gazed upon the body of their only son, Mrs. Blackstone noticed the chain and pendant their son had worn daily since the age of sixteen. The words on the medal read, "Choose Life!"

The Blackstones knew that Matthew was a staunch pro-life supporter; however, the phrase took on a whole new meaning on this particular day. The grieving parents turned to each other, gave each other a knowing look, and then kissed their son for one last time.

"Have you made a decision?" asked Dr. Korbet. "Yes," replied Mr. Blackstone as he dabbed his eye with a tissue. "Matthew would want us to chose life. Our son has no use for his bodily organs now. If they can help someone who needs them, then use them."

Mrs. Blackstone added, "We have one request though. I want the recipients to have our name and address in case they wish to contact us." Dr. Korbet nodded and replied, "I understand." Months later, a large yellow envelope from the hospital arrived. Mr. Blackstone ushered his wife to the couch so they could open the curious envelope together. Carefully, Mrs. Blackstone released the envelope's contents with her heirloom letter opener. Out slid four letters.

The first was from Dr. Korbet. His letter read, " Dear Mr. And Mrs. Blackstone, your son, Matthew's precious gift has given life to eight people who would have otherwise died. Of those eight, these few wished to personally thank you. Best regards, Dr. Korbet." The Blackwells took a deep breath and proceeded to open the next letter. It read, "How can one say thank you for what has been a tragedy to you? Through your son's death, however, my once failing heart now beats strong, and my life-long desire to become a teacher can now be a reality."

Mrs. Blackwell squeezed her husband's hand, and began to read the next letter out loud, "I have not been able to see my three-year-old daughter's face, or gaze upon a beautiful sunset because of my diseased eyes. Thank you and Matthew for the gift of sight! Life is so beautiful, and I will enjoy it to the fullest!"
A sense of serene comfort washed over the Blackwells as they opened the last letter. It read, "I am twenty-one years old, and for most of my life I have been sickly and in and out of hospitals. As I was raised an orphan, and thus had no one to truly care about me, yours and Matthew's gift of life has been the first time I have ever experienced real love. I can only imagine how hard it was for you to make this decision, but rest assured, I will put my new lungs to good use. Your gift of love has given me new hope! Love, Karen"

Tears of both loss and joy began to flow from the Blackstones' eyes.

The reality of organ transplant enables one who has died to give life. While this Daily Wisdom may appear to be about the importance of organ donation, its deeper purpose is to show you, the reader, through example, how Jesus Christ died so that we too may have life. While an organ transplant may improve the condition of the physical body, Christ's gift of eternal life enlivens the spirit. Choose Christ, and choose life!

The Truth About Mediums

"The nations you will dispossess listen to those who practice sorcery or divination. But as for you, the Lord your God has not permitted you to do so."
-Deuteronomy 18:14

A few weeks after my brother died, I was informed by a family member that a relative had gone to see a "medium." A medium is a person who claims to call upon the spirits of the dead, and to see into the future. Upon expressing my disapproval over this negative occult practice, I was told, "Oh, it's just for fun! It can't hurt just to listen."

My friends, there is nothing funny about disobeying God.

In the Bible we are clearly told, *"Do not practice divination or sorcery."* (Leviticus 20:6)
We are also told, *"Let no one be found among you who sacrifices his son or daughter in the fire, who practices divination or sorcery, interprets omens, engages in witchcraft, or casts spells, or who is a medium or spiritist or who consults the dead. Anyone who does these things is detestable to the LORD, and because of these detestable practices the LORD your God will drive out those nations before you. You must be blameless before the LORD your God"* (Deuteronomy 18:10-13)

It CAN hurt even "just to listen" because the Bible tells us that we will be defiled by affiliating with such persons.

"Do not turn to mediums or seek out spiritists, for you will be defiled by them. I am the LORD your God." (Leviticus 19:31)

Most mediums claim that their ability to predict the future or talk with the dead is a gift from God. What makes no sense is that, if this was a Divine gift, then why would God tell us He would basically turn His back on those who involve themselves with this aspect of the occult?

"I will set my face against the person who turns to mediums and spiritists to prostitute himself by following them, and I will cut him off from his people." (Leviticus 20:6)

Some people who have visited such "psychics" insist that the medium told them things no one else could possibly know. My friends, do not be deceived, for the Bible also cautions us that there will be deceiving spirits in the latter days. *"The Spirit clearly says that in later times, some will abandon the faith and follow deceiving spirits and things taught by demons."* (1 Timothy 4:1)

"They are spirits of demons performing miraculous signs, and they go out to the kings of the whole world, to gather them for the battle on the great day

of God Almighty." Revelation 16:14

Some people may involve themselves in things which are an abomination to God because they do not know what God requires of His children.

If you are or have been involved in any aspect of the negative occult, God is willing and able to offer His mercy and grace to those who call upon Him in sincere repentance.

Know God, and know His truth.

Predestination?

$\mathcal{W}$hen someone dies, can this be regarded as their "fate"?

While some people typically accept predestination of believers in God and His son, Jesus Christ, to heaven, many of these same individuals also believe that predestination to hell always involves man's free will so that man, not God, is ultimately responsible for his own damnation. Interestingly, those who adhere to this view also tend to believe that even the "predestined faithful/believers" can also fall away from the faith.

"In love he predestined us for adoption through Jesus Christ, according to the purpose of his will, to the praise of his glorious grace, with which he has blessed us in the Beloved" -Ephesians 1:5-6

"In him we have obtained an inheritance, having been predestined according to the purpose of him who works all things according to the counsel of his will" -Ephesians 1:11

The truth of the matter is that the Bible speaks of both free will AND predestination. It speaks of certain events that were predestined, such as Christ being predestined to come to earth, knowing He would be crucified, die and buried, only to rise again. The Bible also mentions certain people who were born with a handicap, or who became very ill, and some of these were predestined as well.

The reason?

To somehow glorify God; whether by a miracle healing taking place, or to show believers that even when man is faced with adversity, faith in God can allow us to not only over-come, but to actually have peace and joy.

"And they went forth, and preached everywhere, the Lord working with them, and confirming the word by the signs that followed" -Mark 16:20

Another support for predestination is that the Bible mentions that the names of the saved are already written in the *Lambs Book of Life*.

"Only those will enter whose names are written in the Lamb's book of life." -Revelation 21:18

Meaning, even before we are born, God knows who will or won't accept Him. The Bible also mentions that God knows the hour of our death. However, this does not always mean that God will always initiate this death. For example, a teen on drugs may slit his wrists and die. Does this mean this teen's death was predestined; chosen by or planned by God?

No. Man also has free will.

In this example, the teen is using drugs and killing himself under his own free will.

Would God chose or predestine a child to be kidnapped, raped by a molester, then brutally murdered, or was this child a victim of another man's free will?

Since God has, at times, used predestination, and there is also of course, free will, ultimately, we have no way of knowing for certain if a life event is caused by fate (predestination), thus having some greater purpose or deeper meaning than what we are currently aware, or if man has created his own fate through his own choices or free will. However, what we CAN know is that it is God's desire for ALL men to be saved, "... *God our Savior, who wants all men to be saved and to come to a knowledge of the truth*" -1 Timothy 2:3-4, and it is His desire for man to live abundantly. "*The thief [satan] comes only to steal and kill and destroy; I have come that they may have life, and have it to the full.*" - John 10:10

Must I forgive?

"Be merciful, even as your Father is merciful. Judge not, and you will not be judged; condemn not, and you will not be condemned; forgive, and you will be forgiven; give, and it will be given to you; good measure, pressed down, shaken together, running over, will be put into your lap. For the measure you give will be the measure you get back." Luke 6:36-38

"*T*hat witch! I will never forgive her!" blurted Norma as tears streamed down her face.

The person who Norma regarded as best friend had betrayed their friendship, and this caused Norma enormous heart-break.

Years later, Norma was not only holding on to the same anger and bitterness, but the refusal to forgive her former friend had also begun to take a negative toll on her physical and emotional health, causing Norma to suffer from depression, heart-palpitations and ulcers. More importantly, however, Norma's pastor had warned her about the spiritual consequences of her refusal to forgive.

"Norma," he said, "If you will not forgive others, God will not forgive you. If you want

God to be merciful with you, then you must be willing to show mercy to others."

Norma was slow to accept this truth because she believed that people can only forgive those who directly ask for forgiveness, and Norma's former friend had never approached her or ever indicated she wished for such mercy to be shown to her. As such, the pain and hurt which Norma carried with her, and which expressed itself in anger and bitterness continued to grow with each passing year of her life.

My dear friends, forgiveness is not something we only do for others, or even because it is the right thing to do according to God's sight.

Forgiveness is also a gift of love to ourselves.

Contrary to what Norma believed, forgiveness does not necessarily have to mean a relationship with those who our forgiveness is directed toward. One mother of a murdered child told her daughter's attacker on the day of his trial and conviction that she forgave him, and that she will trust God to deal with Him justly, for she refused to allow his act of murderous aggression destroy her as well.

This mother understood that issuing forgiveness does not suggest the act is somehow okay or not severe. Issuing forgiveness is like saying, "Yes, you have sinned, but I am also aware that I too have sinned within my life. Yes, what happened was wrong and hurtful, but carrying that pain with me for the rest of my life will hurt me even more." In other words, forgiveness is a positive step forward, and whose message is, "I want to move forward and not be stuck in the destructive mire."

Has someone hurt you?

Love yourself and God enough to say good-bye to past pain, anger, hurt and bitterness, and hello to the peace and serenity only forgiveness can provide.

"Heavenly Father, please help me to be strong enough to see through my pain so that I can forgive others the way you have forgiven me with my own transgressions. Help me to be merciful to others, the way you, dear God, have been with me. Come in to my heart, God, and show me your love and grace.

This I ask in the name of Your son, Jesus Christ. Amen."

Don't Forget to Wash!

"Blessed are those who wash their robes, that they may have the right to the tree of life and that they may enter the city by the gates. Outside are the dogs and sorcerers and fornicators and murderers and idolaters, and every one who loves and practices falsehood." -Revelation 22:14-15

*H*arry decided to drive for miles and miles. He had some vacation time left, and decided to just drive until he became tired. After nine long hours of driving, Harry was exhausted, and was ready to get a hotel room, take a shower, and eat. Upon trying to get a room, however, Harry was told that although they could offer him a bed and food, none of their rooms had baths. Harry could not believe his ears! He went to every motel and hotel in the small town, and it was the same story each time. In a state of extreme bewilderment, Harry slowly walked down main street, scratching his head and trying to figure out how on earth people were expected to stay clean if they could not bathe. As he strolled in to the more populated main thoroughfare, Harry could not believe his eyes and nose! There was a reeking odor in the air, and the men, women and children he passed on the street were utterly filthy!

Harry felt like he was going mad! He simply could not understand how or why this could happen. It was as if they didn't even realize what an awful state they were in.

In a state of shock, Harry ran to his car and sped off, driving nine hours all the way back home. Exhausted, Harry climbed into his nice clean bed, and immediately fell in to a deep sleep.

"Harry," a voice said, "What you just saw today is what I see on a regular basis. People may use soap and water on their bodies, but as you know, we are more than just physical beings. They remember to use deodorant and soap, but their hearts, minds and souls remain impure due to the rancid effect of sin. You do not see this, but I do, for I see beyond the flesh and into man's very essence. I have provided a way, through My son, Christ Jesus, that man may be cleansed of his sins and purified, but sadly, man often prefers to turn a deaf ear to this truth. The end result is death."

Harry opened his eyes. The room was filled with the bright morning sun.

"Man! What a dream that was!" he said out loud. "I can't wait to tell everyone about it; it seemed so real!"

From that moment on, Harry was a changed

man. For once in his life he fully understood the destructive effect of sin. It was now his new goal to share what he had learned with others.

For Harry, the above story was a dream, but Christ's love and mercy to those who call on Him in repentance is real!

Grow Up!

"When I was a child, I spoke like a child, I thought like a child, I reasoned like a child; when I became a man, I gave up childish ways." -1 Corinthians 13:10

When my children were younger, while my husband and I gave them various chores to do around the house so they would learn responsibility, we understood that their abilities could only go so far. However, when they became teens, I expected more from our children because I knew their level of maturity had increased.

Now that Aaron and Lindsey are now nineteen and twenty, their dad and I hold them to greater accountability.

So too does our Heavenly Father understand that, with the passing of time, should also come an increase in learning, wisdom and knowledge, for man cannot stay a babe forever.

Unfortunately, some of us may grow in body and years, yet there is little change in maturity of mind. I am sure we all may know someone who makes the same mistakes year in and year out, blaming their misfortunes on others, and refusing to take responsibility for their own actions and behaviors.

My dear friends, today is the day to grow up and set aside that part of us whose immaturity is keeping us away from God and godliness.

Stand Firm!

"Indeed all who desire to live a godly life in Christ Jesus will be persecuted, while evil men and impostors will go on from bad to worse, deceivers and deceived. But as for you, continue in what you have learned and have firmly believed, knowing from whom you learned it and how from childhood you have been acquainted with the sacred writings which are able to instruct you for salvation through faith in Christ Jesus." -2 Timothy 3:12-13

*S*ometimes in life we just have to do the right thing, even when it means that doing so will expose us to persecution, or cause us to lose friends.

Of course, it isn't always easy to stand up for what is right, but within my own life, I have found that with truth comes freedom. For example, have you ever been in a situation where someone you know keeps on purposely hurting you with little verbal jabs? Sure, you might take it for as long as you can, but when the time comes, doesn't it feel good to finally say what is on your mind, and to let the person know you will not tolerate that hurtful behavior anymore?

What happens though, when, while standing for truth and righteousness, those persecuting us refuse to see the error of their ways? Do we continue being a door mat, and allow them to jab us over and over again?

To know the answer to this, all we need do is re-read the above Bible verse which instructs us to continue in what we have learned and firmly believe, because our faith is not based within our own word, but Christ Jesus'. Our spiritual reward for standing firm will be great. The above verse is directed to God's children; those who already believe and have studied His word. If you are not yet a believer, before you can stand for what is good and right, you must know what is God's word and will. The only way to do this is to first make a relationship with our Heavenly Father.

"Dear God, I have been trying my way for so long, and it just doesn't seem to be working out well. I am ready to try Your way, and to replace the darkness within my life, with light. I repent of my past sins, and I am ready to start anew. I invite you into my life to be my Lord and Savior. This I ask in the name of Your son, Jesus Christ. Amen."

Be Happy With What You Have

"You shall not covet your neighbor's wife. You shall not set your desire on your neighbor's house or land, his manservant or maidservant, his ox or donkey, or anything that belongs to your neighbor."
                                                -Deuteronomy 5:21

As the above Bible verse conveys, we should be content with what we have and not covet those things our neighbor has that we do not.

Why do you think this is?

Of course God wants us to reach higher and make the best lives for ourselves, but what we may regard as the best is not always what God holds as important. For example, we may love our spouses, and yet we might compare them to an attractive neighbor, or the lady at the grocery store, or the man on the cover of the sports magazine. "If only my wife lost 30 lbs., then we'd have a better relationship," you may say. Or you might think, "Hmm. How much happier my life would be if I had more money!" Or you may say in conversation, "Oh! What I would give to drive one of those fancy European sports cars!"

Once again the question begs to be asked, why

some people, rather than count the blessings they already have, focus instead on what they don't have, or what could be bigger and better. It is nice to want the best things in life, but let us not forget that what God considers important and good are not always the things which hold priority with mankind. Gold, diamonds, furs, fancy cars, big homes and spouses with the bodies of Adonis and Venus hold no relevance to God, or to our walk with God. Certainly God wishes us to be in good health and to prosper, but it is the nourishing and riches of our spirit that matter most to God.

Today, won't you consider placing material and shallow things to the wayside, and ask God to instead bestow upon your heart the desire to richly feed your spirit instead?

One Way

"Salvation is found in no one else, for there is no other name under heaven given to men by which we must be saved" Acts 4:12

A man was driving in a town he was not familiar with. When he turned left down a narrow street, a young woman walking along the sidewalk waved her arms and pointed to a sign which read "one way." Disregarding the woman's caution, the driver proceeded on, only to find himself being shouted at by another passer by. "There is only one way down this street!" an elderly man bellowed. "You are going the wrong way!"

The driver continued on as he ignored the warnings.

From a spiritual perspective, many of us do exactly the same thing.

In the Bible we are clearly told that there is only one way, and that way to our salvation is through Christ Jesus. *"I am the way, the truth, and the life. No one can come to the Father except through me."* John 14:6

Sadly, despite this truth, many people turn away, refuse to hear, and prefer to believe that there are many doors and numerous ways. Such people may claim to believe in a "higher power," yet when they explain what this force is, it has nothing to do with God and His son, Jesus Christ.

"For God so loved the world that he gave his only Son, so that everyone who believes in Him will not perish but have eternal life." John 3:16

My dear friends, your heavenly Father, God, loves you very much, and wants to have a relationship with you. There is but one door, and it is up to you to go through it.

He Is Merciful

"The Lord is kind and merciful, slow to get angry, full of unfailing love. The Lord is good to everyone. He showers compassion on all his creation." Psalm 145:8-9

*M*any people solely see our Creator as a fire-and-brimstone God who is quick to anger, judge and condemn. While God does hold His children to a certain standard, as the above verse extols, He is a heavenly Father who understands man and his weaknesses even better than we know ourselves. As such, God knows our hearts, and whether our desire is to please Him and do good. Likewise, He also understands when we are hurting and in need of His grace, mercy and comfort during those times we must come to Him in repentance because we struggled or fell.

Just as your earthly father or mother would not just stand there and watch when you fall down and hurt yourself, our Heavenly father is even more loving and compassionate. He reaches His hand out to those who cry out to Him, and He is quick to forgive.

We all have made mistakes in life. Only God is perfect.

If you are a person reading this who thinks
that something you may have said or done is
too much for God to forgive, please know that
He is ready and willing to welcome those who
call upon Him in repentance into His family
with open arms.

Jesus Came To My House
(A poem)

*J*esus came to my house one day. He said, "I
am lost. Can you show me the way? I've taken
a wrong turn while trying to say good-bye to a
friend, she's in the hospital, you see, she's near
the end."
I patted his withered hand, and said,
"Certainly sir. Just follow me in my car, and I'll
take you to her."
"How sweet of you to go out of your way! One
day you will be repaid."

Jesus came to my house, he wasn't what I
expected to see; a tiny child who had scrapped
her knee. "There's blood running down my leg,
and into my sock! While riding my bike I must
have hit a rock!"
"No problem, my dear, I said with a smile.
We'll call your mom, and she'll be here in a
little while."

Jesus came to my house, and it was quite a
surprise, for he looked like my bother, the one
who would tease me unmercifully, and call me
"four eyes!" From childhood on he would mock
my face; tease me about my pimples, and never
let me win a race. The story was the same as
we became adults; nothing I could do was
right, and everything was my fault."

"I've come to tell you I'm sorry," he said as he looked at me, "I know I've been unkind, and I ask you to forgive me."

In my mind the painful scenarios ran. I didn't know if I could forgive this bully of a man. A verse from the Bible then gave me a new view. It stated, "*Be kind and compassionate to one another, forgiving each other, just as in Christ God forgave you.*" -Ephesians 4:32
I took his hand and I said, "Of course, dear brother. Christ instructs us to love one another."

<u>Real life application:</u> Many people wrongly think all they need do is pay homage to God and His son, Jesus Christ. However, as the above story suggests, and the below Bible quote affirms, God's light and love is not meant to be held within ourselves, but rather, it is to be generously shared with the masses.

The Christian message does not simply consist of words, but rather, it is a state of being; how we live and give. The love God gives us to give to others is not just for our immediate families and friends, but is for all people; those we know, and those we do not know. It is for the young businessman in the expensive suit who drives the fancy car, and it is for the filthy homeless man who sits in the gutter holding a bottle of cheap wine.

God's love and mercy is for everyone.

"Then he will say to those on his left, 'Depart from me, you who are cursed, into the eternal fire prepared for the devil and his angels. For I was hungry and you gave me nothing to eat, I was thirsty and you gave me nothing to drink, I was a stranger and you did not invite me in, I needed clothes and you did not clothe me, I was sick and in prison and you did not look after me.'
"They also will answer, 'Lord, when did we see you hungry or thirsty or a stranger or needing clothes or sick or in prison, and did not help you?'
"He will reply, 'I tell you the truth, whatever you did not do for one of the least of these, you did not do for me.'
"Then they will go away to eternal punishment, but the righteous to eternal life."

-Matthew 25:41-46

Please God, Not Man

"Be careful how you live among your unbelieving neighbors. Even if they accuse you of doing wrong, they will see your honorable behavior, and they will believe and give honor to God when he comes to judge the world." I Peter 2:12

$\mathcal{M}$any people, at one time or another, deal with gossiping friends, neighbors, and associates. Peacefully co-existing with such individuals who like to spread rumor or malicious lies can be a challenge, as the above Bible verse suggests. Even if you are wrongly accused and the topic of a hurtful falsehood, let your focus be on God so that your behavior continues to be an honor and blessing to Him. This makes great sense since, after all, if we are expending precious time and energy needlessly worrying about silly whispers behind our backs by those who may have issues of their own, then our focus is being taken off God. It is satan and those who are against or anti-Christ that want us to waiver in and neglect our faith.

The other reason why God reminds us to continue in honorable behavior is that our lifestyles can be great tools in reaching those who most need to witness Gods peace, love and wisdom. We can lead by example.

It is easy to be good when everything is going our way, but it is not so simple a task when one is being unfairly treated. While your first inclination may be to return negative jab for negative jab, God calls us to rise to a higher standard.

No, you should not worry about what others may be maliciously whispering, but please DO be concerned that godly living and behaving is what you continually strive for.

Who Is Your God?

"No one can serve two masters. Either he will hate the one and love the other, or he will be devoted to the one and despise the other. You cannot serve both God and Money." Matthew 6:24

$\mathcal{H}$ave you ever been in a predicament where you had to make a choice between doing the right thing and doing the popular or accepted thing? Sometimes it is easy to chose what we know God would want us to select, yet other times, we may wrestle between flesh and spirit. For example, a hostile driver runs us off the road and shouts obscenities at us. While your immediate reaction might be to curse right back at him, or to vindictively issue him the same aggression he bestowed upon you, this initial reaction is not how God would have us behave. The secular world may tell us its okay to return jab for jab, hate for hate, and violence for violence, but as the above Bible verse reveals, if we have made a decision to serve God, then we must honor this choice always, not only at times when it is convenient or easy for us. If we drift in and out between the two; the ways of God, and the ways of man, then whom do we serve?

Like a loving spouse, Christ requires our faithfulness, not just on Sundays or holy days, or when we know someone is watching.

If you are a Christian who is trying to please both God and man, won't you consider recommitting your life to your first Love, Christ?

If you have never made this commitment, what better day to take a firm stand than today?

How Do You See?

I don't like to admit this but I've been feeling a little down lately.

It seems that in the media recently there has been one case after another of children missing, murders committed, and portrayals of senseless violence.

Being a caring person, it is not uncommon for me to shed a few tears, even over complete strangers, and to wish that I could assist these people and their families some way. And so, this last week or two, I have felt a drop in my spirit; a discouragement over how low mankind can sometimes stoop.

This morning, something I said to a family member came to my mind. You see, this relative was having a hard time forgiving another relative of something done nearly thirty years ago. During our discussion this person dredged up numerous negative memories of her dealings with this other person. All she focused on were the sad times; periods when this other person had not lived up to her expectations, or may have reacted to her in a way that was not as warm or patient as she would have preferred.

My response to her was this, "Yes, I know you carry some hurts with you regarding this person, but is it really fair to only focus on her negative traits? What about also recalling the happier times; moments when this person made you feel loved, cared for and special? Can you be fair enough to also look at the positive side of her, and not just the negative?" The person responded, "I've never thought of it that way. I'll try to do that!"

As I ponder this matter and apply it to my own recent emotions over mankind's often violent and cruel streak, I realize that, like this relative, I am not being fair. I am only looking at one side of the coin, and judging the whole of civilization unfairly. I am focusing on the negative acts, and not putting forth the same effort to see that many people do reach out in love.

I have since come to the conclusion that newspaper and television is not the best place to hear about positives. After all, the media tends to prefer to report on issues that hold great drama, and as such, hearing about a boy scout who helped an elderly woman cross the street, or a lady who gave all the money in her purse to feed a homeless man does not typically make exciting news headlines.

There is an old saying that goes something like, "If you look for the evil in mankind, you will find it, but if you look for the good in man, you will find that as well." Shame on me for briefly forgetting this truth.

In similar manner, if we turn our backs on God, He will seem very distant. However, if we seek Him and His truth, there will be no denying His reality.

Is God All-Loving?

*S*ome people believe that God loves and forgives everyone. However, is this true? In the Bible we are told, "*Behold, I am coming soon, bringing My recompense, to repay every one for what he has done. I am the Alpha and the Omega, the first and the last, the beginning and the end.*" (Revelation 22:12)

The above verse clearly reveals that man will not only be eventually judged by God, but this judgment will be based upon the life man has lived.

Robert was a convicted pedophile and murderer who sat on death row in one of the nation's toughest prisons. He was tough, unrepentant, and, showed no indication of remorse, even after ten years. "If given the opportunity, I'd do it all over again!" he snarled. "There is no God, and if there is, He sure ain't no friend of mine," he continued. Those who adhere to this false belief that God is all-loving and therefore will judge no one, may insist Robert will be spiritually rewarded with eternal life, regardless.

The truth of the matter is that God loves everyone who obeys Him, and He forgives those who repent of their sinful and evil ways.

In the above purely fictional story, Robert had
no relationship with God, had no desire to
please the Lord or to do what is good in His
sight. He was totally unrepentant.
God's love and forgiveness are not
unconditional.

*"See, I have set before you this day life and good,
death and evil. If you obey the commandments of
the Lord your God which I command you this day,
by loving the Lord your God, by walking in His
ways, and by keeping His Commandments and His
statutes and His ordinances, then you shall live and
multiply, and The Lord your God will bless you in
the land which you are entering to take possession
of it. But if your heart turns away, and you will not
hear, but are drawn away to worship other gods and
serve them, I declare to you this day, that you shall
perish."* (Deuteronomy 30:15-19)

God desires our worship because He is worthy
of it. He loves us and wants us to love Him in
return, but sadly, not everyone chooses to.
Those who love God enough to allow their
lives to reflect what is in their Hearts will be
rewarded with eternal life, and those who hate
God and His good ways will be eternally
condemned to Hell.

Don't Be A Fool

"The fool says in his heart, 'There is no God.'"
-Psalm 53:1

"There is no God," said Janice to her friend Marge. "If there was, my marriage would not have fallen apart, my mother would not have died of cancer last year, and life would not be so difficult." Marge offered her friend a gentle smile and placed her arm around Janice's shoulder.

"No, Janice, God is real. However, do you want to hear something funny?" Marge asked her sorrowful and frustrated friend.

"What's funny?" asked Janice as she lifted her head up.

Marge replied, "Why do people always blame God when things don't go their way? After all, how do we know it's not Satan causing the problem, or maybe even our own actions?" "God could have stopped my mother from dying!" Janice snapped. "He didn't have to let my husband leave me for another woman either!"

Again Marge gently smiled as she patted her friend's knee. "Your mom smoked for thirty years, sweetie. Even when the doctor told her to stop because she was having trouble breathing, your mom chose to continue. I know you miss her terribly, but do you really think it is fair to blame God for the wrong choices she made?"

Janice shrugged.

Marge continued, "When Henry left you for another woman, did God tell him to do it, or was it Henry's own decision?"

A tear rolled down Janice's cheek as she whispered, "I guess it was Henry's own actions."

Marge patted Janice's knee again as she replied, "That's right, sweetie. Many of the hardships we go through in life are a direct result of our choices, or the choices of those near and dear to us. Sometimes their wrong choices or sinful behaviors end up hurting us though." Marge continued as she reached for her friend's hand and grasped it tightly. "God loves you, Janice. He loves the sacred bond of marriage too, and I am sure it broke His heart as much as yours when you and Henry divorced. And, when your mom died, I am sure He understood your grief, and wanted to comfort you."

Janice placed her hand over Marge's, smiled,

then whispered, "I feel like such a fool now. Thank you for reminding me that there are some things in life we just don't have control of, and that just because bad or sad things sometimes happen, it doesn't mean that God doesn't exist."

The two friends quickly gave each other a warm embrace.

Thanks, God!

*W*ith each passing year of my already
twenty-year long marriage, I am more keenly
aware of just how good God has been to me,
and how thankful I am for all He has blessed
my life with. Oh sure, there have been some
low points, but why focus on life's weeds,
when its flowers are so much more fragrant
and pleasing?

Today's Daily Wisdom does not contain any
quaint stories or profound Biblical lessons. In
fact, rather than for me to TELL you
something, I am going to ASK you something.

I ask that you think about what you are
thankful for.

Sometimes in life it seems like we are always
looking for something; hoping to gain or profit
in some way. Rarely, however, do we think
about how we can give to others.

Saying thank you to those who have blessed us
in some large or small way is a beautiful gift
from the heart which doesn't cost anything,
and yet, which is tremendously precious.
As parents, we remember to tell our children to
pick up their toys, and not to forget to wash
behind their ears, but when was the last time

you told your little ones just how thankful you are for them?

As a wife, I know it is easy to remind our husbands to cut the grass, and to not throw their dirty socks on the floor when they come home from work, but think of how astonished your spouse would be if you turned to him or her while you sat on the couch tonight, and said, "Honey, I just want you to know that I am very thankful I am married to you!"

Think of how many people you can make smile today just by letting them know how much you appreciate them.

Did a stranger hold the door open for you as you entered the mall today? ("My, what a gentleman! Thank you!")

Did the driver in your left lane let you pass him? (Thanks a heap!)

Did a friend email you a cute poem or ditty? (Thank you for thinking of me!)

Most importantly, let us not forget to thank God for creating the world, and allowing us to live upon it. Let us thank Him for the gift of being a mother, father, grandma or grandpa, friend, sibling, and loving spouse. Thank Him for the food on our tables, and the roofs over our heads. Let us give thanks that we have

clothes to wear and are reasonably healthy.
Thank Him for our jobs, and our modern
conveniences, because in some places of the
world, there are people who have none of
these.

Lastly, let us thank our heavenly Father for the
free gift of salvation to all who believe in God
and His son, Jesus Christ.

Thanks, God!

The Counselor

A young man tells a counselor the heart-breaking story of a loved one who he believed was a Christian. This person's involvement with street drugs eventually caused so much damage in this that she now even doubted God's existence, and wanted nothing more to do with his friend or other Believers.

The counselor thought for a moment, rubbed her chin, and then calmly replied: "I must tell you that I tend to believe that those who truly love God with all their hearts and souls are not so quick to totally reject Him. Mind you, I believe it is possible for those who genuinely love God to become lost, deceived and fall in to sin and deception for a while, but whether it is a week, month, year or more, those who truly love God come back to Him once the truth of their sin reveals itself in full to them. As such, if your loved one truly did love the Lord, she will again come back to Him. If she doesn't, she probably never really did."

Looking confused and frustrated, the young man pondered this response, then replied, "Maybe so, but you don't know this for sure. You are only stating what YOU believe."

"Allow me to explain why I believe this," stated

the counselor as she nodded knowingly. "If a heart is truly filled with love for God, our desire will be to please HIM, and to put HIS wishes first, rather than our own. Once sin reveals itself, if we continue on in sin, we are, in essence, telling God that He is not Lord in our life, and that our way and desires are held in higher esteem than are His. You and I have no way of truly knowing what exactly your loved one's relationship with God was, but more importantly, how is it NOW?"

For the remainder of the session, the counselor went on to offer helpful advice to the young man.

Today's Daily Wisdom is not solely about the dangers of drug use, but rather, to assist those who are hurting in any way, shape or form, whether it be those addicted to drugs or alcohol, involved in pornography, involved in adultery, hateful mind-sets, and any other type of evil that is negatively affecting one's life and relationship with the Lord.

Whether you are seeking to know God and His better way, for the first time, or if you are a Believer who has fallen in to a place of ungodliness, God's love, grace and mercy is just waiting to wash over you so that you may start anew.

A Brand New Day

"Christ has given each of us special abilities-
whatever He wants us to have out of His rich
storehouse of gifts." Ephesians 4:7

s the silver-haired woman walked up the long drive, she could see him peering through the window. Every day it was the same thing; she would come to clean up the house and he would just sit there in his wheel chair staring out the window. Oh, he could speak alright, but I suppose he simply chose not to. And who could blame him? Ever since the accident five years ago, the once familiar faces that used to fill this large home with life began to slowly drift away, much like his once positive attitude.

"Good morning, sir", Helen, the housekeeper stated as she walked through the door. Charles, the thirty-five-year-old paraplegic whose domicile it was, grunted.

"Cat got your tongue again today, sir?" retorted Helen coyly as she began to put away the dishes on the counter.

Again Charles simply grunted and continued to stare out the window.

The day progressed and Helen went about dusting, polishing, sweeping and washing. It was a particularly dreary afternoon due to what seemed like an all-day rain. Feeling her mood drop a little, and knowing how much a good ditty raised her spirits, Helen turned on the radio, going from station to station in an effort to find just the right song. Just as she found a lively polka, suddenly a loud roar pierced the melodic tones coming from the radio.

"Turn that garbage off!" demanded Charles, his face contorted with anger.

Helen was so caught off guard by the sudden strong display of emotion that, in her attempt to quickly turn the radio off, she accidentally broke the nob completely off. With polka music now blaring, Helen momentarily stood expressionless. Then, all of a sudden, her lip began to crinkle, then tremble, and from the depths of her belly came the most delightful and prolonged laugh! Glancing over, Helen could not believe her eyes! Her wheel chair-bound boss was also chuckling heartily!

Upon composing themselves and unplugging the radio, Charles used his eyes to motion for Helen to come near him. Helen knelt near his wheel chair to ensure that they could face one another.

"I am so very sorry for yelling at you, Helen", stated Charles as he stared intensely at the elderly woman's face. "I don't know what came over me, not just at that moment, but ever since I've been a prisoner to this wheel chair. Hearing the music was yet another cruel and painful reminder of what I have lost, and never will have again.

Helen didn't say a word, but merely held Charles' limp hand and listened.

"At one time I used to love music, dancing, reading, and the arts in general. All of that died when I became paralyzed. Look at my life now. I have nothing."

Tears began to roll from Charles eyes. Helen let go of Charles' hand, and began to dig through her purse, immediately grasping a tiny framed picture.

"Look at this picture, and tell me what you see", she quietly asked Charles as he looked at her puzzled.

"It's blank. Nothing is there. It's just white", replied Charles.

Helen smiled subtly, and said, "Oh no, sir. It is a beautiful snow fall, or perhaps it is a fluffy white cotton ball, or a crisp white bed sheet hanging outside on a line outside to dry." She continued, "That picture is like ones life. Either it can remain a blank canvas, or we can make something beautiful and meaningful out of it. The choice is ours."

"No, said Charles, I didn't have a choice. My choice was stolen away!"

Helen smiled again and quietly replied, "I beg to differ, sir. You still have choices, but you just need to be a bit more creative by digging a little deeper, so that you can see what those choices might be."

Charles now clung to her every word. "I don't understand what you mean. Please explain." Helen thought a moment; then her eyes lit up. "You like music and dancing, right, sir?" "No, I USED to enjoy dancing to good music!" abruptly stated Charles.

"No, sir, if you loved it once, you will still love it, but remember what I said; be creative!" stated Helen assuredly, and she moved his one good finger over the switch that made his electric wheel chair move. She then walked over to the radio and plugged it back in to the wall, the robust polka music still playing. Up and down went the click of Charles' switch, and back and forth went his wheel chair. Charles smiled richly, then clicked the tiny lever to the right, then left, and round and round went his wheel chair!

"Look, Helen! I'm dancing! I'm dancing to the music!"

Helen nodded, grinning from ear to ear as she reached over to momentarily stop Charles' chair from moving two and fro.

"There's more, sir", stated Helen. "Remember how, before your accident, you always used to say that you loved being around little children because they were so full of promise? Well, there is no reason why you can't still live out that dream by being a little creative. You may not be able to push a child on a swing at the play ground, but the local library has been searching high and low for someone to fill the part-time position of storyteller in the children's reading room."

For the first time in a very long time, within Charles eyes, Helen could see life and hope. She did all she could to keep herself from crying at that moment; however, these would be tears of joy.

With new, bright eyes, Charles asked, Helen, "how did you get to be so wise?"

Helen looked down to her arm, and slowly began pulling up her sleeve, soon to reveal tiny numbers permanently marked on her skin. "You see, sir, when I was a little girl, my entire family died in a concentration camp. I was the only survivor, and I had no one, not even an aunt or uncle. Like you, I felt like I had everything important taken away from me, and my future seemed very bleak. A kind couple adopted me shortly after that, and while I still missed and loved my family, I came to also love them. They showed me that we all are special in God's eyes, and that we also have special gifts that we need to discover and use so that we can help others. It is this circle of giving and receiving that life is all about. Through this I was able to experience joy again."

Helen then reached into her purse again to fumble with the tiny framed picture.
"They are the ones who gave me the tiny white picture many years ago, and before I left for college they told me that what that picture reflects is up to ME."

Charles sat motionless, once again staring momentarily out the window, then stated with newfound resolution, "Helen, tomorrow is going to be a brand new day; the beginning of my new life!"

Spiritual application: As the above Biblical verse reveals, Christ has given each of us special abilities and it is up to us to use these gifts for the good of mankind. For some people, that gift might be the ability to be a teacher, good public speaker, author, doctor or nurse. For others, it might be someone who has a special way of dealing with and helping people. Perhaps your gift is to be a day care provider, or retired grandparent who volunteers time at the local community center helping young children to swim. Regardless of what our life circumstances are, God's desire is not for us to abandon these gifts merely because times may get tough. Instead, as the above story reflects, He wants for us to be creative and to find ways to continue on giving in one form or another so that He and His Word may be glorified.

Tomorrow CAN be the beginning of a brand new day!

About The Author

Melanie **Schurr** is a former columnist for

the *Colorado Daily* newspaper, and a multi-published free-lance writer whose works have appeared in numerous newspapers, magazines, and electronically. She has written articles on child-care, spirituality, and self-help. Schurr is the author of *SON Salutations, Daily Contemplations,* and *Ecstatic Living/Ecstatic Loving: A Christian marriage manual and life-guide.* The 47 year old wife and mother of 23 yrs. is a 10+ year weekly contributing writer for *Daily Wisdom,* (www.DailyWisdom.com) which, up until recent, was sponsored by *The Gospel Communications Network,*

(www.Gospelcom.net), the most popular
Christian web site on the world wide web. She
typically assumes the Saturday time slot, and
her inspirations strive to lead the reader to a
deeper relationship with God. It is not
uncommon for readers to contact the author
for informal advice and prayer, and for Church
educators world-wide to seek reprint
permission for use in sermons, Bible studies
and newsletters.   Visit the author's personal
web site at MelanieSchurr.com, or purchase
her books online at Barnes and Nobles,
Amazon, and BooksAmillion.

Contact the author at Editor@MelanieSchurr.com